Dr Calabro,

Hope you are

doing well

We figured

it would

only appeal

to baseball fans.

Turned out

we had a

marketable play

we didn't see

coming

Let me know what

you think

OUT!

a play in two acts

by

Lawrence Kelly

Published by Windsor House Publishing
New York, NY
Library of Congress Cataloging-in-Publication Data
Kelly, Lawrence.
        Fade to Black/Out! : A play in 10 scenes about the
    1919 Black Sox scandal.
        1 p.
    ISBN 9781453840115
    PAu0007785651 1985-10-31

www.outtheplay.com

OUT! was first presented by the PACT Theater Company at the Judith Anderson Theater in New York City in June, 1986.The production was directed by Max Charruyer; the settings were by Michael Deegan; the costumes were by Sarah Conly; the lighting was by John Conway. The cast was as follows:

"Shoeless" Joe Jackson .... MICHAEL COUNTRYMAN
Oscar "Hap" Felsch..RICK TOLLIVER
Claude "Lefty" Williams... TERRY HEMPLEMAN
George"Buck"Weaver... RICHARD TABOR
Arnold "Chick" Gandil .... PAUL CHRISTIE
Charles "Swede" Risberg.. ARNIE MAZER
Eddie Cicotte... STEVEN STAHL
Fred McMullin .... JOHN A. O'HERN

OUT! was subsequently presented by the Philadelphia Theatre Company at the Plays and Players Theater in Philadelphia, Pennsylvania in June 1987. The production was directed by Sara Garonzik; the settings were by Peter Harrison; the costumes were by Vicki Esposito; the lighting was by James Leitner. The cast was as follows:

"Shoeless" Joe Jackson .... PETER MORSE
Oscar "Hap" Felsch.. GRANT SHAUD
Claude "Lefty" Williams... TERRY HEMPLEMAN
George"Buck"Weaver.. JONATHAN FULLER
Arnold "Chick" Gandil .... MATTHEW PENN
Charles "Swede" Risberg.. ARNIE MAZER
Eddie Cicotte... TOM TETI
Fred McMullin .... PATRICK GARNER

TIME: Fall 1919 to Fall 1920
PLACE: Chicago, Illinois USA

Act I
Scene 1: Fall, 1919, Chicago Locker Room
Scene 2: Playing Field, during the next week
Scene 3: Locker Room
Scene 4: Hotel Room

Act II
Scene 1: Playing Field, during the World Series
Scene 2: Locker Room, after the third game
Scene 3: Locker Room, after the World Series
Scene 4: Fall, 1920, locker Room
Scene 5: Courtroom/Locker Room
Scene 6: Playing Field

For Dawn, my wife, and Dan D, my life long friend, who in one of our many heated discussions blurted out, "Sports isn't an activity! It's a way of life!"

AUTHOR'S PRODUCTION NOTES

Each director brings his/her own personal touch to each production.
I have brought few suggestions to the creative process. What I have
concentrated on is the sound of the play. In conception, there was clear
musicality to the words that I heard in my head. This play is a barrage
of different ideas, points of view and emotions that is thrust on the
audience. As such, pacing is a vitally important consideration during
production. All locker room scene dialogue should fly. The energy of
the actors should be optimum. I have suggested to actors that when they
are in the locker room, they are not actors, but reactors. Cues should
be picked up immediately and no pauses should be inserted. There
are no one-liners in the play and any humor that occurs is the result
of the character's commitment and not from the wit of the writing.
The badinage should be at break neck speed as anyone would attest
who has spent any time in locker rooms. I have not yet witnessed a
production that ran too quickly, but I have witnessed the dreariness of a
production that ran too slow. The monologues and other scene settings
are opportunities for individual instincts. In the locker room, the "team"
is one entity, albeit, with many voices.
Nudity is also a question that is brought to me during production. After
all, this is a play set in a locker room where actors change their clothes
more often than models backstage at a runway fashion show. Nothing in
the script or stage direction addresses nudity. I have left it to individual
theaters and individual creative teams to make their own determination.

Universal praise for *OUT!*

"Captivating!" 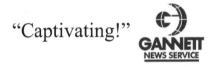 GANNETT NEWS SERVICE

"Intriguing!" **The New York Times**

"Compelling!" TIME

"Wonderful!" *NEW YORK POST*

"Explosive!" THE CHRISTIAN SCIENCE MONITOR

"Exceptional!" **San Jose Mercury News**

"Thought-provoking!" **The Philadelphia Inquirer**

"Touches all the bases!" **DAILY NEWS**

In 1919, the Chicago White Sox were heavy favorites to win the World Series. They didn't. This is their story.

There are three working areas of this play. One is a locker room which consists of a long row of lockers, benches, stools, water fountain, baseball bat rack and anything else one might see in a baseball locker room. Another is just a black stage which serves as the practice and playing field during games. The last area is a dark hotel room with a couch, chairs, lamps and other items seen in a hotel room. The players will make all costume changes right onstage, switching from baseball uniforms to street clothes to baseball uniforms and back. This play consists of a series of scenes and also quite a few monologues in which the players come downstage and address the audience. The action is continuous with an intermission after Act I, Scene 4.

(The following is an example of the opening of the play from one production. Directors are free to begin the play according to their creative vision.)

The play opens in black and underneath we hear the song "Swanee" sung by Al Jolson. A car horn beeps then the song changes to "Prohibition Blues" followed by industrial sounds and a version of "How Ya Gonna Keep Down On The Farm". As the light changes to a gray or sepia tone a movie screen drops. Before the screen finishes it's descent a newsreel begins to flash on it. The title: "News Of The Day—1919" flashes up on screen. Then: "Paris Peace Conference Continues With The Big Three" and footage comes up of Woodrow Wilson, David Lloyd George, Vittorio and Georges Clemenceau conferring. Cut to: " In Sports Charles Comiskey says his White Sox Will Win World Series" and actual footage of a White Sox game in 1919 and then shots of Comiskey standing with members of his team. As Comiskey smiles each player/actor is in close up in matching newsreel footage.

Act I Scene 1

At the top of the play we see the locker room, empty at first and then the PLAYERS enter periodically as the dialogue begins. Before THEY enter, we hear the sounds of a baseball game in progress and of thousands of fans responding to what they see on the playing field. There is the sound of the ball hitting a bat, fans cheering, fans booing, etc.

JACKSON

I'm Joseph Jackson. I was born in 1887 in Brandon Mills, South Carolina. My first full season of major league baseball was in 1911. I batted .408. I'm good. Some people say the best. I played twelve years. Got out in 1920. I was hitting .382. I'da hit 400 again.

FELSCH

I'm Oscar Felsch. I was born in 1891 in Milwaukee, Wisconsin. My first year in baseball was 1915. I was a starter in the outfield when Joe Jackson came over from Cleveland that same year. He was good. I thought he'd take my job away. Luckily we got to play next to each other. I left baseball in 1920. I was having my best year.

WILLIAMS

My name is Claude Williams. When I was young back in Aurora, Missouri, kids used to call me Clod Williams . That was until I started playin' baseball. You couldn't call a guy a clod who was striking you out all day. I started major league ball in 1913 with Detroit. They didn't play me much over there. When I came here in 1916 I got to pitch. I was pretty good. I was no Christy Mathewson but I was good. I won twenty-three games in 1919 and twenty-two in 1920. Only problem was my teammate Eddie Cicotte won twenty-nine. So who got all the press? I never played anymore after 1920. I was just reaching my prime.

WEAVER

I'm George Weaver. I was born in 1891 in Stowe,
Pennsylvania. I never played for any other team
than this one. Came up in 1912. Started every year.
I played third base. Little shortstop, not much.
I was goddam good. Good as Honus Wagner,
I thought. No one else did though. He never
impressed me. If I'da played longer I'da been just
as good. I was hitting .333 in 1920. Never hit that
high before.

GANDIL

I'm Arnold Gandil. I was born in 1888 in St. Paul,
Minnesota. I came up with this team in 1910. I had
a bad year so they got rid of me fast. Shipped me
to Washington. It was my first year. You think they
would have waited a while to see if I developed.
No chance. You gotta produce. Did good with
Washington. Did real good. They got me back here
in 1917. Probably the best move they ever made.
One thing I am is a winner.

RISBERG

I'm Charles Risberg. I was born in 1894 in San
Francisco, California. I only played four years in
this league. All with this team. If you ask me it
was four years too much. I was an okay player. I
never kept track of that stuff. I just played. What's
baseball? It's a dumb game anyway. People think
I'm crazy. I just want to be left alone. I like Gandil
though. He's got class.

CICOTTE

My name is Edward Cicotte. I was born in 1884 in
Detroit, Michigan. I've been playing baseball for as
long as I can remember. When I was a kid I used
to hang out all day at the General Store and look at
these picture cards of baseball players. My favorite
was Cy Young. Everybody liked Cy Young. Even
my dad liked Cy Young. So I made a vow to

CICOTTE(Continued)

myself. Someday I was gonna be as good as Cy Young. I took my knife and carved a big circle on a tree we had in the backyard and found myself the roundest stones I could find and threw them at that circle all day long, every day. The best I did was 147 in a row. I led the American League in wins in 1917 and in 1919. I been in the major leagues fifteen years. I'm the oldest guy here. I'm not a leader though.

(THEY ALL break and go to various positions on the stage to begin the play, except JACKSON who comes forward and addresses the audience)

JACKSON

All hell broke loose in September of 1920 . . .

GANDIL

It wasn't so bad.

WILLIAMS

It just happened.

RISBERG

Shit on 'em.

JACKSON

The biggest news of the year wasn't the war being over. It wasn't prohibition. Nope. It was what happened to us. The Chicago White Sox. And it all started in the fall of 1919 . . . Good game, Eddie.

CICOTTE

Thanks, Joe.

WEAVER

We wupped 'em.

JACKSON

We did. We did.

CICOTTE

I felt good.

WEAVER

You goddam pitched goddam good.

CICOTTE

Well I felt good. What I was trying to do was . . .

WEAVER

Who cares what you were trying to do. We won.

JACKSON

I thought we were gonna give it to them in the
fourth.

WILLIAMS

The fourth was shaky.

WEAVER

What happened to Chick? Hope it's all out of his
system.

WILLIAMS

Chick was shaky.

WEAVER

Well I hope it's out of his system. But no matter.
We got goddam "Shoeless Joe" Jackson. Whooeeyl
Three for four, four rbi's!
     (Mock seriousness)
Joe ... you're a goddam inspiration.

CICOTTE

Joe was good.

WEAVER

Yes he was. Yes he was.

JACKSON

Yeah.

FELSCH

(Aside to GANDIL)

You played an excellent game today, Chick.

GANDIL

Thanks, Hap.

FELSCH

I didn't play too good today. I've put a lot of thought
into it and I think it's just a matter of timing. I'm
reading this book which tells that if an athlete is
not mentally prepared to participate in an athletic
event that his motor reflexes will not correspond to
the action that is taking place within that particular
event. It's all a meeting of the mind and the body.
You see, the mind has got to be connected to the
body. I just don't think I had the right outlook today.

GANDIL

You were shit today, Hap.

FELSCH

Well . . .yeah...I suppose... that's basically what I'm
trying to say.

RISBERG

(To WEAVER)

Don't use my bat.

WEAVER

Sorry. Mine broke.

RISBERG

That's not my problem. Don't use my bat.

WEAVER

What's the big deal? I only used your goddam bat.

RISBERG

You only used my goddam bat? A bat is a very
personal thing. It has its own feel to it. It's a part
of me. When I grab my bat I know exactly how it
should feel and weigh. I'm familiar with it.

WILLIAMS

I know what you're talking about, Swede. I get the
same feeling when I grab my joint.

RISBERG

Stuff it, Williams.

JACKSON

Swede, lighten up.

RISBERG
(To WEAVER)
Don't use my bat.

WEAVER

Okay.

FELSCH

You can use mine, Buck.

HEAVER

Thanks, Hap.

WILLIAMS

Hey, Joe, I always wanted to ask you. How'd you
ever get the name "Shoeless"?

JACKSON

I don't quite remember.

WILLIAMS

You must remember how you got a nickname.

GANDIL

Go ahead, Joe, tell him.

JACKSON

It's no big deal.

WILLIAMS

I want to know.

GANDIL

Come on, Joe. Tell him. He wants to know.

JACKSON

It's not important.

GANDIL

Okay, I'll tell him. Years back when Joe first came
up with Philadelphia, they were on a road trip and
Joe misplaced his shoes and socks in his hotel
room...

JACKSON

I didn't misplace them. Someone stole them.

GANDIL

Whatever.

JACKSON

I was a rookie. They thought it was funny.

GANDIL

Anyway when he gets on the train to leave he's all
dressed except he's completely barefoot. They all
start yelling, "Hey, Shoeless Joe!" It stuck ever
since.

WILLIAMS
(Laughing)
How could you lose your shoes, Joe?

JACKSON

I didn't lose them. Someone stole them!

WILLIAMS

Right. That's funny.

CICOTTE

(Laughing a little too much trying to join GROUP)
It sure is.
(To WILLIAMS)
How'd you get the nickname Lefty?

WILLIAMS

(Dumbfounded)
Because I'm a lefty.

FELSCH

(To RISBERG)
I think you were being a little hard on Buck, Swede.
We should be concerned about achieving comradery.
We've just about got the pennant wrapped up. Now
is when we should be concerned with getting closer
together as one team, not arguing and instilling
animosities that are going to draw us apart. Don't
you agree, Swede?

RISBERG

Felsch, do me a favor, will you?

FELSCH

Sure, Swede, what?

RISBERG

Get the hell away from me.

WEAVER

Anybody know what Cleveland did?

JACKSON

I heard they won.

FELSCH

I heard they lost.

MCMULLEN

They play tomorrow.

WEAVER

Hey, Chick, what the hell happened to you today?

GANDIL
(Defensively)

What do you mean?

WEAVER

I threw those two balls to you in the fourth inning chest high. You dropped them both.

GANDIL

Oh yeah. I'm real sorry. I had something in my eye.

WEAVER

They gave me an error on the throw on the second one. It hurt my stats.

GANDIL

I had something in my eye. I said I was sorry. Who gives a shit about your errors.

CICOTTE

Anybody see that dame in the first row behind home plate?

(No one answers}

CICOTTE (Continued)

Did you, Joe?

JACKSON

No I didn't.

CICOTTE

She sorta ruined my concentration. Every time I pitched I saw her right over Schalkie's shoulder. All I could think about was sticking my head right smack in the middle of those two big titties. She was beautiful. Did you see her, Weaver?

WEAVER

No.

CICOTTE

How 'bout you, Williams? See her?

WILLIAMS

Nah.

CICOTTE

McMullin, you saw her, didn't you? She was beautiful.

(Exits)

MCMULLIN

She was butt ugly.

FELSCH
(To MCMULLIN)

You didn't get in again today.

MCMULLIN

Nope.

(Takes swig from flask in locker)

FELSCH

You should lighten up on the hooch, Fred. You been hitting that thing for weeks now. You're lucky you didn't get in today. You've been tanked since this morning.

MCMULLIN
Mind your own business, Hap.

FELSCH
Just trying to help, Fred. I care about you. I don't
like seeing you do this to yourself.

MCMULLIN
Go read a book on it.

(FELSCH turns away)

MCMULLIN (Continued)
Hap . . .

(FELSCH turns and looks at MCMULLIN)

MCMULLIN (Continued)
Thanks . . .

(FELSCH smiles)

WILLIAMS
What are you doing this afternoon, Joe?

JACKSON
I got to go over to Sisters of Mercy and visit all the
sick kids. I made a commitment.

WILLIAMS
God, every time I turn around you are going to the
hospital, visiting the sandlot games or signing balls
for the poor kids. You get paid for all that stuff?

JACKSON
Noooo. Just give my time. What are you doing
today?

WILLIAMS

Me and the missus are having a little cookout at the house. It's my little boy's birthday. I was gonna ask you to bring the wife and kids.

JACKSON

I'll be done at the hospital around 5:OO.

WILLIAMS

Well, come over when you're done. We'll still be there.

JACKSON

All right.

WEAVER

What are you batting now, Joe?

JACKSON

.367

WEAVER

Goddam. I can't seem to get above .300. I've been around .295 all year.

JACKSON

Your own bat might help.

WEAVER

Yeah.

RISBERG
(To GANDIL)
We made out pretty good.

GANDIL

Yep.

RISBERG

You gonna talk to Jackson today?

GANDIL

Shut up.

RISBERG

No one's listening.

GANDIL

Shut up.

WILLIAMS

Fred, you got five bucks you can lend me?

MCMULLIN

No.

WILLIAMS

Come on. I'll pay you back this week.

MCMULLIN

I said no.

WILLIAMS

Swede, how 'bout you? You got an extra five you can lend me?

RISBERG

You're a professional ballplayer. You're supposed to be rolling in cash. You don't have five bucks?

WILLIAMS

I work for Charles Comiskey, remember. If he paid me a lot of money how is he supposed to be a wealthy man?

JACKSON

We do okay.

WILLIAMS

Who does okay? We win the World Series two
years ago and he cuts our pay. Says it's our way to
help fight the Huns. Hell, I don't even know what a
Hun looks like.

WEAVER

It's for the war. Everybody pitched in. Things could
be worse.

WILLIAMS

Not much. Come on, can anybody lend me five
bucks?

JACKSON

Here, Lefty.

WILLIAMS

Thanks, Joe. I'll get it back to you as soon as I can.

WEAVER

We win the goddam World Series that's about five
grand, fellas!

FELSCH

What's the losers' share?

CICOTTE

Around three grand.

WEAVER

What are you talkin' losers?!   It's in the goddam
bag.

FELSCH

You never can tell, Buck.

WEAVER

Sure I can. We got the best goddam team in
baseball. We're gonna do it.

JACKSON

Tell 'em, Buck.

CICOTTE

We'll do it.

WEAVER

You bet your ass we will. And when we do that's
five thousand dollars a man. Every man. Even Mac.
And he hasn't played in a month.

CICOTTE

He'll get in. We're saving 'em. Right, Fred?

MCMULLIN
    (Unenthusiastically)
Yeah.

WEAVER

Speaking of money. Chick, I want to know what
kind of contract you got. First baseman must make
a lot more than third baseman. Look at you. Fancy
suits, silk shirts. Where the hell you get all the
cash?

WILLIAMS

He's going down on Comiskey's old lady.
Commy don't know about it. He meets her at the
Businessmen's Club after the games and they go
over her box scores.

JACKSON

Have a little respect. She's a fine woman.

WEAVER

What gives, Chick?

GANDIL

I have what you call brains, lard head. I know about
investments.

WEAVER
You know about something.

WILLIAMS
What time's batting practice tomorrow? I've got to get a move on.

FELSCH
Eleven o'clock.

WILLIAMS
I'll catch you guys later. My wife's having a cookout this afternoon.

FELSCH
I'll go with you, Lefty. We'll split a taxicab.

WILLIAMS
I've got my speedster.

FELSCH
Oh.

WILLIAMS
You need a ride?

FELSCH
If it's not too much trouble.

WILLIAMS
No, not at all.

FELSCH
Great. So . . . you're having a cookout?

WILLIAMS
Yeah, it's my kid's birthday.

FELSCH

That's nice. You'll be cooking frankfurters and
hamburgers, I suppose?

WILLIAMS

We planned on it.

FELSCH

That's great.
    (Pause)
I love frankfurters and hamburgers.
    (Pause)
I bet you'll have a great time.
    (Pause)

WILLIAMS

Hap, would you like to come over this afternoon?

FELSCH

Are you inviting me?

WILLIAMS

Yeah, I'm inviting you. Would you like to come
over?

FELSCH
    (As THEY BOTH exit)
Gee, that's great, Lefty. But I can't today, I'm busy.

    (THEY exit)

JACKSON

Where are we off to next week?

WEAVER

Philadelphia, first. Then on to Boston. Goddam, I
love Boston.

JACKSON

Nice city.

WEAVER
The best. I know a girl in Boston.

JACKSON
You know a girl in Boston?

WEAVER
Yep.

JACKSON
What about your wife?

WEAVER
She won't mind.

JACKSON
She won't mind?

WEAVER
No. She likes her.

JACKSON
She likes her?

WEAVER
Yeah, a lot.

JACKSON
She knows about her?

WEAVER
Yeah.
        (JACKSON looks amazed)

WEAVER (Continued)
It's her sister.

JACKSON
You get a kick out of funnin' on me?

WEAVER
(Laughing)
Sorry, Joe. It's just so goddam easy.

RISBERG
(To GANDIL)
You want me to stick around?

GANDIL
Yeah, hang out a bit, okay?

WEAVER
Hey, Chick, now that you're looking so sharp, you want to go with me and chase a few skirts?

GANDIL
No.

WEAVER
Come on, It'll be fun.

GANDIL
I went with you once. I've had more fun on the toilet bowl.

WEAVER
How bout you, Fred?

MCMULLIN
No.

WEAVER
Joe. What about you?

JACKSON
I can't, Buck. I have to get over to Mercy.

WEAVER
Well . . . I guess this farm boy drinks alone.

(No response)

WEAVER (Continued)
I'll head out then. .367, huh, Joe? Goddam.
(Starts to leave)

RISBERG
Hey. Weaver.

WEAVER
Yeah, Swede, did you want to go . . .

RISBERG
Don't use my bat.

WEAVER
'Night, Joe.

CICOTTE
I'm heading out, Buck. I'll have a drink with you.

WEAVER
(As THEY leave)
All right.

CICOTTE
Great!

WEAVER
You know, I'm not in the mood for a drink anymore,
Eddie. Maybe I'll just go home.

CICOTTE
Come on, Buck! Just one.

(JACKSON sits off to the side finishing dressing. There is a long silence
while RISBERG looks at GANDIL and GANDIL looks at RISBERG
and THEY BOTH look at MCMULLIN who doesn't notice because
HE's off in his own world. After a while RISBERG nudges toward
GANDIL to get on with it. GANDIL walks slowly toward JACKSON)

                    WEAVER
What say, Joe?

                    JACKSON
Not much, Chick.

                    GANDIL
How's the wife?

                    JACKSON
Fine.

                    GANDIL
Good. The kids?

                    JACKSON
They're just dandy.

                    RISBERG
        (Trying to help out)
You got two great lookin' kids there, Joe.

        (GANDIL looks at RISBERG)

                    JACKSON
Yeah.
        (Long pause)

                    MCMULLIN
(Senses what's going on. Chuckles to himself near
locker)
How's the wife, Joe?

                    GANDIL
Can it.
        (Pause)
Listen, Joe, can I talk to you for a minute?

JACKSON

Free country. Mind if I finish dressing?

GANDIL

No, no, no, go ahead. Well . . . uh . . . well . . .

JACKSON

You ain't sayin' too much there, Chick.

GANDIL

Well, I don't really know where to begin.

MCMULLIN

(Off near locker)

How 'bout "How's the wife, Joe?"

RISBERG

Shut up!

JACKSON

What's with him?

GANDIL

Don't mind him, Joe. He's drunk.

JACKSON

You better lay off the whiskey, Fred. That stuff will
kill you.

MCMULLIM

(Laughs)

It's okay. I can afford it.

GANDIL

Hey, Joe, forget about him.

RISBERG

Yeah, Joe, listen to Chick; he's got something
important to talk to you about.

JACKSON
Well, get on with it, Chick.

GANDIL
Well . . . you like this shirt, Joe?

JACKSON
Yeah, it's pretty snazzy.

GANDIL
It's silk, Joe. Imported.

JACKSON
It is one snappy shirt.

GANDIL
You know how much a shirt like this costs, Joe?

JACKSON
I'd say quite a bit. 'Round four dollars.

GANDIL
Seven dollars, Joe.

RISBERG
You ever see Chick's auto, Joe?

JACKSON
Yeah. Top of the shelf stuff.

RISBERG
You know what I bought my wife for our
anniversary, Joe?

JACKSON
I can't say that I do.

RISBERG
A diamond necklace, Joe. Diamonds.

JACKSON

That's right generous of you, Swede.

MCMULLIN
(From locker)
Ever see my silver flask, Joe?

GANDIL

Shut up.

RISBERG
(Goes to MCMULLIN)
You say one more word and I'm gonna turn you into mincemeat.

GANDIL

You ever think of owning things like this, Joe??

JACKSON

Nah. Can't afford it.

GANDIL

Maybe you can. Maybe I can help you out.

JACKSON

You guys make some investment, is that it? You want me to put some money into a chicken farm or something?

GANDIL

No. Nothing that difficult. This is ten times easier.

RISBERG

And a sure thing.

JACKSON

Well, what the heck is it?

GANDIL

Well . . . it's pretty evident we got the pennant sewn up.

JACKSON

Yeah.

GANDIL

Well, we're a sure thing to get into the World Series.

JACKSON

A sure thing.

GANDIL

. . . I've got some friends that would pay pretty handsomely for us to uh well . . . let's just say . . . not be at our best.

JACKSON

If you're suggesting what I think you are you better button it up right now, Chick.

RISBERG

Hear him out, Joe.

GANDIL

There's no harm in just hearing what I have to say, Joe.

JACKSON

I know what you have to say! I hear what goes on. You want me to blow the World Series!

GANGIL

Not completely blow it. Just make a few mistakes, that's all.

JACKSON

You want me to go out there during the World Series and make some errors for a little money?!!

RISBERG

What's wrong with that, Joe?

GANDIL

Wake up, Joe. It's happening all around you. I can
name you ten guys off the top of my head that have
been doing it for years. Why shouldn't we get a
piece of the pie?!! The people in the stands are
getting rich off us. I think we deserve a little of that.

JACKSON

For a little money!!

GANDIL

I don't think you completely understand what I'm
talking about here. I'm not talking about a little
money, I'm talking about good sums of money.

RISBERG

Joe, you have a son. What happens if he can't play
baseball? Do you want him to work in a factory
or something? Don't you want him to have an
education? You ain't got no education, Joe. You
know it's been rough for you. Do you want it to be
that rough for him? Here's how you can get him that
education.

JACKSON

Get away from me. What you guys are talking about
is wrong. It's illegal.

GANDIL

But it's beautiful, Joe. And it's not illegal. Think
about it. How can anybody prove it? We made some
errors, that's all. How do they know if it was on
purpose or not?

RISBERG

If we all keep our mouths shut there's no way they
can prove anything. It's foolproof.

JACKSON

It's wrong.

GANDIL

Is it wrong for me to be wearing this shirt? You
have eyes, Joe. Look. I have nice clothes, my own
auto. You didn't know where it came from. Is that
wrong?

JACKSON

You've been involved already?

GANDIL

A little. Not too much. So has Swede.

RISBERG

Lefty, too. And Fred.

MCMULLIN

And I don't even play.

JACKSON

I don't want to hear any of this. I said get away from
me.

GANDIL

Just think on it, Joe. You don't have to give us your
answer right now. We'll talk some more.

JACKSON

My answer is no.

RISBERG

Think of your kids, Joe.

JACKSON

I said no!

RISBERG

We're talking a lot of money.

GANDIL

Come on, let's leave him alone. Just think about it,
Joe. That's all we ask.

RISBERG

We need you with us, Joe.

JACKSON

Well, you won't have me with you!

GANDIL

I said leave him alone.
    (As HE and RISBERG are about to leave)
Come on, Fred, let's go.

MCMULLIN

I want to stay for a while.

RISBERG

(Lifts MCMULLIN up by shirt)
He said let's go.

MCMULLIN

(Pulls away)
I want to stay for a while!

GANDIL

Leave him, he's drunk.
    (RISBERG lets go)

GANDIL (Continued)

All right, Joe, we'll talk to you soon, okay, Joe?

JACKSON

There's no reason to! I said no!

RISBERG

Have a good night, Joe.

GANDIL

(Stops at exit as THEY are about to leave)
Uh, Joe. If you don't go in on it, we'll understand.

JACKSON

I'm not going in on it!

GANDIL

There's absolutely no risk. You now know about
us. Could you play the World Series with us next to
you? Join us, Joe. We need you.

JACKSON

Get the hell out of here!

(BOTH exit. Just JACKSON and MCMULLIN are now left Onstage.
BOTH are involved in their own thoughts. MCMULLIN still sits
drinking from his flask and after a while JACKSON slowly rises and,
finishes gathering up his gear. THEY do not speak or notice each other
until JACKSON breaks the silence. Pause)

JACKSON (Continued)

I've got to get over to the hospital.

(JACKSON walks toward the exit , looks at MCMULLIN, wants to say
something, then decides not to. Continues on toward the exit. Stops.
Turns, looks at MCMULLIN and says . . .)

Hey, Mac?

MCMULLIN
(Never looks at JACKSON)

Yeah?

JACKSON

Why did you get involved?

MCMULLIN

(Gets up, and walking away from JACKSON without looking at him,
says in a heavy, drunken Irish accent)

For the thrill of it, me boy. For the thrill of it.

(JACKSON stares, then slowly turns and exits. MCMULLIN sits for a while, then slowly rises, walks toward the audience as the lights dim behind him. When HE starts his monologue HE has his flask with him and is still quite drunk)

MCMULLIN (Continued)

Why did I get involved? At first I was a bit flattered. I mean Fred McMullin is not a name that will be etched forever in the major league baseball record books. I'm what you call a utility player. I can play six different positions. None of them very well, mind you. To be approached to make errors for money when all my efforts were put into trying to catch the fuckin' ball in the first place was quite humorous. I was not blessed with natural ability. I've had to work twice as hard as any player in the league and I have been half as successful. My whole life I've seen players attack this game with such ease and grace . . . and I've had to work! . . . struggle . . . put in extra hours . . . maintain total concentration . . . just to attain an average level. And I might add, an average salary. Money . . . money . . . yeah, I needed the money. My little girl . . . consumption. It was Lefty who first approached me. He said Chick had it all worked out. My little girl was sick. It was rough on my wife. I was away from home a lot. My wife had to carry most of the burden. I figured I could send home some extra cash. Get the best doctors . . . give her the best treatment. And I did . . . I mailed it home . . . my wife didn't even know where it came from. I took every penny and sent it straight to my wife . . . special delivery . . . My baby died . . . I justified what I was doing with my little girl . . . Her life was being saved . . . I could convince myself . . . then she was gone . . . but I was still involved.

(Walks slowly out)

BLACKOUT

Scene 2

As the scene opens we see JACKSON Downstage pantomiming
shagging fly balls in the outfield. GANDIL appears on the opposite aide
of the stage of JACKSON and slowly takes a long cross to JACKSON.
This scene is stylistic and meant to show a passage of time in which the
simple action happened time and again.

GANDIL

What do you say, Joe?

JACKSON

Scram!

GANDIL

Looking good, Joe.

JACKSON

Get lost!

GANDIL

(To audience)
See, I knew I could break Joe. I just couldn't leave
him alone. Every day I'd approach him. He'd be
shaggin' some flies, takin' some swings, whatever.
He was gettin' all confused. It was affecting his
game. I knew I was gettin' to Joe, when he wasn't
playin' good.'
(To JACKSON)
I just think you're making a big mistake, that's all.

JACKSON

Get the hell away from me. I'm not telling you
again!

GANDIL

Don't be a fool, Joe. What are you, after all? You're
someone's property. That's what a baseball player is,
property. Comiskey owns you. Just like he owns that
German Shepherd of his. Yeah, you're valuable

GANDIL (Continued)

to Comiskey now. But in a few years when your legs start to go, you see how fast he ships your ass out of here.

(RISBERG enters)

GANDIL (Continued)

I'm not talking about a little money.

RISBERG

It's foolproof.

GANDIL

Think of your wife, Joe. You love her, don't you? Sure would be nice to make a little extra cash. So she could enjoy herself a little bit.

RISBERG

Think of your kids, Joe. We're talking about a lot of money here.

GANDIL

I'm not talking about a little money. I'm talking about great sums of money.

RISBERG

It's foolproof.

JACKSON

I don't know, I don't know.
(Hits ball. ALL stare)

JACKSON (Continued)

I owe Comiskey.

                    GANDIL

What do you owe Comiskey?! What's he ever done
for you? What are you gonna get for all your years
in baseball? A lot of records in some book . . . that
you can't even read. You're sure not gonna be
rolling in clover.

                    JACKSON

You'll get caught.

                    GANDIL

It's not illegal.

                    RISBERG

It's foolproof.

                    JACKSON

I don't know. I don't know.

                    GANDIL

Just think on it, Joe.
     (Exits)

                    JACKSON

I'm thinking! I'm thinking!

                    RISBERG

Joe. Everybody knows Ty Cobb makes three times
the money you do.

     (JACKSON stares at RISBERG)

               BLACKOUT

Scene 3

As the scene opens we see the PLAYERS involved with getting suited for the game that is about to be played. THEY are ALL there chatting amongst themselves.

(Dir. note: A lot of the locker room banter is left to improvisation and the discretion of the director, but ultimately THEY should eventually resort back to the text.)

WILLIAMS

What's that, Hap?

FELSCH

Just a book I'm reading.

WILLIAMS

What's it about?

FELSCH

It's a psychology book.

WILLIAMS

(Looks at book)
Dale Carnegie. Any good?

FELSCH

It has some very interesting theories. It's helped me understand myself and have more confidence.

WILLIAMS

Yeah?,

FELSCH

I think so.

WILLIAMS

Understand yourself, huh? You like reading all that stuff?

FELSCH .
I find most of what I read quite helpful.

WILLIAMS
No kidding? Think I could read that stuff?

FELSCH
Sure. I don't see why not.

GANDIL
Stick to the funny papers, Lefty.

WILLIAMS
I could read that stuff. Couldn't I, Hap?

FELSCH
Sure you could, Lefty.

GANDIL
How could you read it? There's no pictures.

WILLIAMS
Listen, Chick. I read a lot of stuff you don't know
about.

MCMULLIN
Sure . . . menus, street signs . . .

GANDIL
Yeah, liquor bottles, cigarette packs . . .

(MCMULLIN and GANDIL enjoy the joke)

WILLIAMS
Very funny.

FELSCH
Don't listen to them, Lefty. Would you like to
borrow this?
(The book)

WILLIAMS
Yeah I would. Thanks, Hap. It works, huh?

FELSCH
It has for me.

WILLIAMS
How many pages is it?

FELSCH
About four hundred.

GANDIL
Four hundred? Next year when you finish it, give it
to Jackson. He shoulda learned to read by then.

MCMULLIN
Four hundred pages? I got a buck that says he
doesn't finish it by next year.

WILLIAMS
You guys should be in those Ziegfeld Follie shows.

(JACKSON enters)

CICOTTE
Hey, Weaver, what the hell happened to your eye?

WEAVER
(A small mouse on his eye)
Ah, I got into a little scuffle at Stacey's Tavern last
night.

RISBERG
You got to stop fighting with the cocktail waitress.

CICOTTE
Stacey serving alcohol?

WEAVER

In the basement. Select clientele.

CICOTTE

What happened?

WEAVER

Oh, some asshole at the bar who was loaded said Cincinnati would wipe the floors with us during the World Series.

CICOTTE

What did you do? Hit him?

WEAVER

No, I didn't touch him. The guy was about seventy years old. I just calmly walked over to him and said that I was Buck Weaver and I could assure him that we were going to win.

CICOTTE

So how'd you get the shiner?

WEAVER

Well, the old bugga turns to me and says, "You're Buck Weaver?" Stuck my chin up and said "Yes, I am"... thought the guy was going to ask me for an autograph or something. All of a sudden he picks up his cane and whacks an inside curve on the side of my face.

CICOTTE

You're kiddin'?

WEAVER

No. Seems the guy lost a sawbuck on our Philadelphia game. Says I struck out with runners on second and third that would have won it.

JACKSON
You didn't strike out in the Philadelphia game.

WEAVER
That's just it. It happened three goddam years ago.
He's been pissed off ever since.

WILLIAMS
You always were a likable guy, Buck.

JACKSON
Lefty, I think my kid's gonna be a pitcher. You
should see him toss the ball.

WILLIAMS
Well, it's the toughest position. You think he's got
the guts?

WEAVER
You've got to be kidding. If it wasn't for real
ballplayers behind you, you guys would be useless.

WILLIAMS
All the pressure's on us. We control the tempo of the
game.

WEAVER
That's a goddam joke. When you're getting
shellacked we're like jackrabbits trying to run after
the balls that they're hitting all over the park.

WILLIAMS
Half the time we're striking so many guys out you
guys could play poker out there and no one would
notice.

MCMULLIN
I play poker and no one notices.

WEAVER .

You pitchers make me laugh. You can't even hit the goddam ball. You have to concentrate on one thing. Throwing the ball over the plate. And most of the time you don't even do that good.

FELSCH

That's not necessarily so, Buck. There's been research that the stress level for a pitcher is three times that of other positions. They actually have possession of the ball twenty times as many times as, say, a third baseman like yourself.

WEAVER

Where do you get all this shit?

FELSCH

I don't know what you mean, Buck.

WEAVER

You're like a goddam encyclopedia. Stress level, three times as many, twenty times as many. Where do you get all this shit?

FELSCH

I read, Buck.

WEAVER

Well, I read too. I never see any of that shit.

FELSCH

Maybe I could recommend some material for you to glance over. It might improve your game.

JACKSON

Watch out for his cane, Buck!

GANDIL

Hey, Lefty, when you finish that book could Buck borrow it?

WEAVER
(Exasperated)
I think I'll go shag some flies.
(HE exits)

CICOTTE
Poor Buck.
(TO JACKSON) .
So you have a budding pitcher on your hands?

JACKSON
He tosses it pretty hard. Only problem is I think he's
a lefty.

WILLIAMS
Nothing wrong with that. Lefties have a higher
intelligence, you know?

RISBERG
So what are you? A freak of nature?

FELSCH
(TO RISBERG)
Actually, Swede, what Claude is saying is . . .

RISBERG
Shut up, Felsch.

JACKSON
There's nothing wrong with him being a lefty. I can
always convert him to an outfielder.

CICOTTE
Like father like son.

JACKSON
Yeah, something like that.

WILLIAMS
(To JACKSON)
Has your kid lost his shoes yet?

JACKSON
No.

WILLIAMS
(Feigning heart attack)
You're kidding? You mean there might be a Jackson
who wears shoes?

JACKSON
Funny. Very funny.

WILLIAMS
I can see it all now. Batting fourth, in left field,
"Spats" Jackson!

RISBERG
(Aside to GANDIL)
I think Joe's bending.

GANDIL
How do you know?

RISBERG
He asked me how much money we were talking
about.

GANDIL
What did you say?

RISBERG
I said he should work that out with you.

GANDIL
Good. Did you talk to him about Felsch?

RISBERG

No. I figured you'd want to do that.

GANDIL

Okay. If we can get Joe I know we can get Felsch.

RISBERG

What about Dickie Kerr?

GANDIL

We don't need him.

RISBERG

You sure? It's another pitcher.

GANDIL

Positive. Forget about him.

RISBERG

What do you want me to do?

GANDIL

Get these guys the hell out of here. Let me be alone with Joe.

RISBERG

Right. What about Cicotte?

GANDIL

If we can get Jackson to convince Felsch, Cicotte will do anything Felsch says.

RISBERG

Right.

CICOTTE

When do we start the big ones?

JACKSON

In ten days. The first one's home.

CICOTTE .

I could really use the dough. Let's win the damn
thing, huh?

JACKSON

Yeah.

FELSCH

On paper we have the better team. I figured it out
man to man and we have the edge over them by at
least four positions.

JACKSON

Baseball's funny.

RISBERG

Yeah, anything could happen.

FELSCH

Well, if no one gets an injury and all of us show up,
I still feel we have it sewn up.

JACKSON

You never can be too sure.

CICOTTE

I could sure use the dough.

FELSCH

Yeah. So could I.

RISBERG

Hap, what say we go out and play a little pepper.

FELSCH

Wow. Gosh, Swede, you never asked me to play
pepper with you before.

RISBERG

I didn't ask you to marry me. Don't make such a
big deal out of it.

FELSCH

I'm just real surprised, that's all.

RISBERG
   (Irritated)
Do you want to play pepper or don't you?

FELSCH

Sure.

RISBERG

Well, let's go.

FELSCH

Let me get my glove.

RISBERG .

Hurry up already, will you. Mac, come on, join us. I
want you to play some pepper.

MCMULLIN

What for?

RISBERG

Don't ask questions, just come on.

GANDIL

Do what he says, Mac.

MCMULLIN
   (Repeating)
Do what he says, Mac.

RISBERG

Hey, Felsch, you almost ready?

FELSCH

Coming.

RISBERG

Well, shake it, for God's sake.

FELSCH

(Ready now)
Gee, Swede, this is great.

RISBERG

Yeah. Yeah.

FELSCH

Mac, you playing too?

MCMULLIN

Got to do what the man says.

RISBERG

See you out there, Chick.

GANDIL

Yeah.

FELSCH

(As THEY exit)
Mac, I heard you might be playing today. Collins is not feeling well.

MCMULLIN

Yeah?

(RISBERG, FELSCH and MCMULLIN exit)

CICOTTE

Strange. Swede asking Hap to play pepper.

WILLIAMS

It's the World Series. It brings guys closer together.

CICOTTE

I guess so.

(GANDIL goes and whispers something in WILLIAMS' ear)

CICOTTE (Continued)
Don't you think it's a little strange, Joe?

JACKSON
I don't know. Maybe Lefty's right.

WILLIAMS
Hey, Eddie, will you come out with me and show
me how you throw that knuckleball of yours.

CICOTTE
Sure, Lefty. I didn't know you were that interested
in my shine ball . . .

WILLIAMS
Oh, I am. I've admired the way you've thrown it for
years.

CICOTTE
No kidding? Well, let me get my stuff .

WILLIAMS
Great. This sure means a lot to me.

CICOTTE
Things are sure getting strange around here.

WILLIAMS
What do you mean?

CICOTTE
(As THEY are about to leave)
Maybe it is the World Series. Let's go.

WILLIAMS

(As THEY exit)

Great. So what do you do? You put your two fingers on the seams like this . . .

CICOTTE

No. No. You got it all wrong.

(WILLIAMS and CICOTTE exit. GANDIL is now alone with JACKSON. After a pause)

GANDIL

Have you thought over what we talked about, Joe?

JACKSON

I haven't thought about anything else.

GANDIL

Swede says you have some questions you want answered. Maybe I can help.

JACKS0N

There's a lot of things that have to get cleared up before I say yes or no.

GANDIL

I agree with you one hundred percent. I want to erase any doubts in your mind. .

JACKSON

Oh, there are a lot of them.

GANDIL

For example?

JACKSON

For example: How much are we talking about here? I mean, if I'm going to put myself at risk I want to know what I'm risking myself for.

GANDIL

That's all negotiable. You name your own price.
The way we work it is that everyone works out their
own deal. This way no one can say they're gettin'
cheated. No one knows what anyone else is making.
It's all kept private. The only one who knows the
exact amounts everyone gets is me.

JACKSON

How can you be sure we won't get caught?

GANDIL

Because I'm sure. No one's going to say anything
because everyone has something to lose. If some
people question our caliber of play, so what? Those
people would question it anyway. We keep it very
tight knit. Only the guys that are involved stay
involved. We don't bring in any others and we don't
talk about it.

JACKSON

It sounds better.

GANDIL

It's not just better, it's great. We need you, Joe.

JACKSON

You know, just because I'm involved, and I haven't
said I am yet, don't mean we're going to lose. I'm
only one guy.

GANDIL

Well, I wanted to talk to you about that. We've
thought about it. We feel, my friends and I, that if
we could convince you to come along with us that
you might be willing to talk to Felsch. This is all
carefully thought out and we feel we can get away
with it with eight fellas.

JACKSON

Hap would never go for it.

GANDIL

Not alone maybe, but he would if you talked to him.
You have a lot of pull, Joe. You're Shoeless Joe
Jackson. The guys look up to you. They respect you.
You could convince any of them. That's why it's so
important that we have you on our side. And we're
willing to pay you accordingly.

JACKSON

Maybe so, but Hap will still be tough.

GANDIL

I'm not too sure about that. You heard him say he
could use the dough. I think all he needs to know is
that you're with us.

JACKSON

Well, I'll tell you what I'll do. I'll talk to Hap. I
don't like it, and I don't know what I'm gonna do
yet, but I could use the money.

GANDIL

You won't be sorry, Joe.

JACKSON

But I'm telling you one thing right now. If I do
decide to go in on it, whatever price I decide on, I
want it in cash. Up front. Or the deal's off.

GANDIL

That can be arranged.

JACKSON

And I swear to you, Gandil. If anything happens. If
anyone slips up. And I go down. I'm bringing you
all down with me.

GANDIL

Nothing's going to happen, Joe. As long as we all
keep our mouths shut.

JACKSON

Let's hope so - - Now get the hell away from me.
You make me sick just lookin' at you.

GANDIL

You got it, Joe. I'll be speaking to you later, right,
Joe?

(No answer)

GANDIL (Continued)

Right, Joe?

JACKSON

Yeah.

GANDIL

I know you'll make the right decision, Joe. Don't
worry about nothing.

(GANDIL exits. JACKSON sits alone pondering what HE has just
agreed to do. HE slowly finishes getting his uniform on and after a while
walks Down towards the audience. The lights behind him dim slightly)

JACKSON

I have a responsibility. I have a responsibility to my
family and I have a responsibility to my fans . . . A
man's job is to provide for his family. In the best
way he knows how. I'm gonna do that.

(Goes to exit. GANDIL is on his way in)

GANDIL

'Scuse me, Joe. I forgot my hat.

JACKSON
(After a pause)
Hey, Chick. Remember what I said. Up front.

GANDIL
Up front.

(JACKSON slowly turns and exits. After a moment GANDIL grabs his hat and walks toward the audience)

GANDIL (Continued)
Joe was a lot easier than I thought he'd be. Funny what men will do for money. I'm always amazed how people will do something they feel is wrong if there are other people doing it. Somehow . . . if there are enough people doing it, it doesn't seem so wrong. God, I love America. Where else can you make an honest dishonest buck?
(Laughs to himself)
You see, this thing is all highly planned out. These guys don't give me any credit for being so innovative. McMullin was easy. Risberg's my pal. He gets Williams. Williams gets Weaver. I get Jackson. Jackson gets Felsch. Felsch gets Cicotte. And we all get rich and live happily ever after. It can't miss. And it isn't that terrible. Fact, it isn't even against the law. You know why? Because the lawmakers never even considered it. I thought it up. Me. Is that genius? I mean, think about it. If it's okay for you to sit up in the stands and make money off me, why can't I be out on the field and make money off me? Am I right? Besides, in fifty years who's gonna care?

(Turns and walks toward the exit. When there HE stops, turns to the audience for the last word before GANDIL exits.)

. . . Certainly not you.

BLACKOUT

Scene 4

The action of the scene opens in the Downstage area of the stage. It's a hotel room, three days before the World Series is about to begin. As the scene opens we see GANDIL, RISBERG, JACKSON, CICOTTE, FELSCH and MCMULLIN. SOME are standing drinking beer, pacing, smoking cigarettes, etc. SOME are seated on a sofa, chairs and the like. GANDIL is the master of ceremonies and THEY are waiting for WILLIAMS and WEAVER.

GANDIL

Who are we waiting for?

RISBERG

Lefty. He's bringing Weaver.

CICOTTE

Let's get this thing started.

GANDIL

We'll give them a while longer.

CICOTTE

Well, let's get going. What if someone sees us?

GANDIL

What if they do? What are we doing? We're eight members of the Chicago White Sox having a pep talk in our hotel room. Will you relax.

CICOTTE

Relax, he says. Hap, I don't know how I let you talk me into this.

FELSCH

Wait a minute, Eddie . . .

GANDIL

Hap . . .

RISBERG

Hey, Cicotte, there's the door. Nobody's twisting your arm. Yet.

CICOTTE

I'm a little concerned, all right?

GANDIL

Just sit down and relax. There's nothing to worry about. All your questions will be cleared up shortly. Let's just wait for Lefty and Buck.

RISBERG

Sit down.

CICOTTE

I feel like standing.

(Pause)

MCMULLIN
(Aside to CICOTTE)
You want a drink?
(Offers flask)

CICOTTE

Yeah. You still gettin' this stuff. You must be paying top dollar.
(Takes a long belt)

MCMULLIN

I got friends.

GANDIL

Where the hell are they?

RISBERG

They'll be here.

GANDIL

You told them four o'clock, right?

RISBERG

I told Lefty. He was going to tell Weaver,

GANDIL

They're late.

JACKSON

Maybe something happened.

CICOTTE

Maybe they changed their mind.

GANDIL

We'll give them a few more minutes.

FELSCH

(To JACKSON)
You're sure this is okay, Joe?

JACKSON

I think so, Hap.

FELSCH

I hope so.
        (Pause)
Nice game yesterday.

JACKSON

Thanks.

MCMULLIN

(Aside to GANDIL)
I hate to be the bearer of bad tidings but don't you
owe me something?

GANDIL

It's coming. It's coming.

RISBERG

Leave him alone, This isn't the time. Go sit down.

FELSCH

(Aside to CICOTTE)

Eddie, you don't have to stay if you don't want to.
I'm not too sure about this thing.

CICOTTE

I don't really mind. If it's square with Joe and it's
square with you then it's square with me.

FELSCH

Well, I'm not too sure this thing is all that square.

CICOTTE

Whatever you decide I'll go along with.

FELSCH

Okay. But, you're a grown man. Just remember it's
your decision.

JACKSON

Hey, Fred, do you have an extra cigarette?

MCMULLIN

Sure.

(Gives him one which JACKSON takes and starts to light)

MCMULLIN (Continued)

I didn't know you smoked.

JACKSON

I do at home. I try not to do it in public. You know.
Set an example for the kids and all that.

MCMULLIN

Oh...yeah. Me too.

RISBERG
What do you mean "me too"? What do you do? Try
not to pass out near playgrounds?

JACKSON
(Takes a long drag and exhales)
Good smoke.

MCMULLIN
Yeah.

CICOTTE
Are we going to start this thing?

GANDIL
Listen, we can't ...

(WILLIAMS enters)

GANDIL (Continued)
Where the hell have you been?

WILLIAMS
Downstairs. There was this organ guy with this
monkey. You should have seen the tricks this
monkey could do. He had his hat in his right hand...

GANDIL
What the hell is wrong with you?

WILLIAMS
What??

GANDIL
Where's Weaver?

WILLIAMS
I don't know. He wasn't with me.

CICOTTE
Shit. This thing's gonna take forever.

GANDIL

Well, we've got to find out if he's with us or not.

WILLIAMS

Buck's in. He's in. But he doesn't want to know anything. He doesn't want to hear anything. He wants to deal through me.

GANDIL

Through you? Fine. If that's the way he wants it. Let's get started. You'll fill him in later.

CICOTTE

Hallelujah.

(EVERYONE gets comfortable as the meeting gets started)

GANDIL

The reason we're getting together is we wanted to get straight amongst us all how we were going to go about this.

FELSCH

Wait a minute. I haven't said I'm going along with this yet.

GANDIL

Let me talk for a while, Hap. Don't interrupt. I'm certain all your doubts will be gone if you let me finish what I have to say. If you have any questions you can ask then afterwards. Now . . . You all must be interested in the idea or else you wouldn't be here. This thing is not some half-baked venture. It's been all highly thought out. The guys that I'm involved with don't fool around. They're professionals. There's too much money involved. The thing is very simple. We make a few errors and get paid for it. How much you get paid is all individual. I'll take you one at a time into the other

GANDIL (Continued)

room and we'll work that out. Now . . . What I
want to stress is that what makes this thing work is
that we all stick together. No one knows about this
except us. And no one is to know about this except
us. You can not tell a soul. Not even your wives.
Especially your wives. I promise you. There is no
way anyone can prove anything if we just keep our
mouths shut. There is absolutely no way that I can
prove that you made an error on purpose, Eddie.
That's what makes this so brilliant. And so easy.
Besides, what's the big deal? We won the series in
'17. Did anyone's life change? Are you better off
now than you were two years ago? Hell, we're in
the same position we were in two years ago. Life
goes on. Does anyone have anything to say?

CICOTTE

I just want to say that I just don't feel right about
this thing. The only reason I'm doing this is because
Joe and Hap are doing it. And I need the money.
What happens if when we go into that other room I
don't get what I want?

GANDIL

I'm sure that won't be a problem, Eddie.

RISBERG

Whatever you get is going to be more than your
share of the Series take if we won.

FELSCH

I'm not quite sure how exactly we're going to make
these errors.

GANDIL

That will all be worked out later. We'll know before
each game what we have to do. Different situations
during the game will mean different approaches.

MCMULLIN

Will I get paid even if I don't play?

GANDIL

Of course. You're in, you get paid.

FELSCH

I don't know.

GANDIL

Well, we've got to know, Hap, if you're with us.
We've got to know if you're all with us. I'm in.
Swede's in. Lefty and Fred are in. Are you Joe?

JACKSON
    (Thinks a second)
Yeah.

GANDIL

Eddie?

CICOTTE

I'll probably be sorry . . . Yeah.

GANDIL

Hap?

FELSCH

Yes.

GANDIL

Great. The only way we can do this is as a team.

RISBERG

Right.

CICOTTE

As a team. Gandil, don't you have any lousy
feelings about what we're gonna do?

GANDIL

Not at all , Eddie. We're in a business. We're
businessmen. There are people in the stands who
are laying odds on every game played. Every inning
played. Some on every pitch that's thrown. What
we're doing has been going on for years. And will
go on for years. It's show business and we're the
entertainers. The fans don't really care if we win or
lose. Just that they're entertained.

CICOTTE

I don't know.

JACKSON

Well, let's get on with this. I have to go umpire a
sandlot game .

GANDIL

All right , Joe. Then why don't we go inside and talk
turkey.

(JACKSON goes into other room)

MCMULLIN

You don't need me. I'm going to get the hell out of
here.

WILLIAMS

Wait, Fred. I'll go down with you.

(MCMULLIN and WILLIAMS exit)

RISBERG

Hold on, guys. Chick, do you want me to stick
around?

GANDIL

Nah, kiddo. All I have to do is talk to these three.

RISBERG

All right then. I'm gonna leave.

GANDIL

All right. I'll talk to you later.

RISBERG

(As HE leaves)
Wait up, guys. You want to go to the track?

(RISBERG exits)

GANDIL

(To CICOTTE and FELSCH)
I'll be right out.

(GANDIL goes into other room. CICOTTE and FELSCH are left
alone in the room. Slight pause)

CICOTTE

Hap? How much are you going to ask for?

FELSCH

Five thousand dollars.

CICOTTE

Five thousand dollars! Will he pay that?

FELSCH

We'll soon see.
(Pause)

CICOTTE

This doesn't sit too well with me, Hap. I've got a
giant knot in my stomach.

FELSCH

I should have never got you involved.

CICOTTE

I know what I'm getting myself into. You're not
holding a gun to my head.

(Long pause)

CICOTTE (Continued)

Don't it bother you, Hap?

FELSCH

Sure it does. But heck, the way I figure it, I can
make in one week the same money I make in two
years.

CICOTTE

Yeah.

(Pause)

FELSCH

How are your kids?

CICOTTE

Great. My little boy's a monster. Can throw the ball
just as hard with both hands.

FELSCH

Maybe he's ambidextrous.

CICOTTE

What the hell are you trying to say?

FELSCH

No, nothing like that. It means he can do things
equally well with both hands.

CICOTTE

Maybe he is. Hell, that would be something.

(Thinks; laughs)

CICOTTE (Continued)

Could you imagine if he grew up to be a pitcher and could throw the ball with each arm? Hell, if you got a hit against him right handed he could turn around and pitch to you left handed.

FELSCH

(Laughs)
I'd hate to face a pitcher like that.

(JACKSON and GANDIL enter)

GANDIL

I'm glad everything worked out, Joe.

JACKSON

Just remember what I told you.

GANDIL

I'll remember.

JACKSON

And, Chick, I mean it.

GANDIL

I know you do. You take it easy. I'll see you tomorrow. Eddie, you want to come in now?

CICOTTE

Yeah.

(GANDIL and CICOTTE go into other room)

JACKSON

I'll see you, Hap. I'm late. I have to go.

FELSCH

Okay. How'd it go?

JACKSON

Fine.

(JACKSON exits.

(FELSCH is alone in the room. HE sits on the bed, ponders for
    awhile, then rises and walks Downstage to the audience)

FELSCH

Eddie asked me if it bothers me . . . it does. You
see . . . I'm a fairly above average ballplayer. I'm
not great . . . I make too many mistakes . . . I'm too
erratic. I try to read books so I can improve but they
really don't do any good . . . I still I make the same
mistakes . . . I don't make much money . . . I like
playing baseball . . . but it's not what I've always
wanted to do . . . This may sound funny . . . but what
I always wanted to do was work with kids. I never
went to college . . . We didn't have much money
when I was small ... My father used to say to me,
"Why you bother with this baseball garbage? Get
a good job" . . . He didn't understand baseball . . .
He's proud of me now . . . So I worked real hard ...
but I always wanted to work with kids ... I need the
money so that maybe I can go to college . . . maybe
get a job working with kids . . . but then I ask myself
. . . would I want my kid influenced by someone like
me?

(GANDIL and CICOTTE enter)

GANDIL

There, now that wasn't difficult, was it, Eddie?

CICOTTE

How will I get my money?

GANDIL

Don't worry about it. We'll get it to you. You'll
know when and where.

> CICOTTE

Okay.

> FELSCH

How'd it go, Eddie?

> CICOTTE

Fine, Hap.

> GANDIL

Come on, Hap. Last but not least.

> CICOTTE

I'll call you later, Hap.

> FELSCH

Sure.

> GANDIL

I hope it goes as smooth for you as it has for
everyone else.

(GANDIL and FELSCH exit. CICOTTE walks to audience)

> CICOTTE

I don't believe it. I looked Gandil straight in the
eyes when he asked me how much. I told him
ten thousand bucks. Figure I'm worth more than
Felsch. You know what his reaction was? Fine. Ten
thousand bucks! That's a hell of a lot of money. I
can save the mortgage on my farm. Get myself a
new auto. Take a trip around the world, hell, the
wife would like that. I just feel a little funny. I don't
know if it's worth it. But hell, ten thousand bucks!
And I been thinking. I won twenty-nine games this
year, I'm supposed to get a bonus if I win thirty.
Comiskey says it's not possible for me to pitch
in the last few games. Something about rotation,
saving my arm for the Series. Makes me wonder. I

CICOTTE (Continued)

went to church after Joe talked to me. I asked the pastor if it was a sin to get paid for not doing your best. You know what he said? He said if you can find someone stupid enough to pay you for being mediocre then "go with God's blessing, my son." I figured, hell, if it wasn't a sin and it wasn't against the law, then it must be okay. But I still have this pain in my stomach. I still feel a little funny.

INTERMISSION

Act II Scene 1

AS the scene opens we see ALL the PLAYERS standing onstage in a straight line singing the National Anthem. After the anthem, they all break and run to their respective positions. WILLIAMS, who is not pitching today, is sitting off to the side with MCMULLIN, who is not playing. CICOTTE is pitching; GANDIL, first base; RISBERG, short-stop; WEAVER, third base; JACKSON, left field and FELSCH, center-field. It is Game 1 of the World Series.

The players stand in a line onstage and sing the last two lines of the Star Spangled Banner,

> ". . the land of the free and the home of the brave . . . "

They break and go to their positions ad-libbing chatter to start the World Series.

> CICOTTE
> I've faced Rath before. Never had any problems with him. He's not a strong hitter. Can run like a rabbit though.

(There is baseball banter all through these scenes)

> WILLIAMS
> Come on, Eddie!

> GANDIL
> Go get 'em, boy!

> WEAVER
> Sit him down, Eddie! Sit 'em down!

> CICOTTE
> Maybe I better throw around him.

(CICOTTE winds up and throws ball toward audience which represents the hitter. After HE throws the ball ALL PLAYERS just stare straight ahead. Not a word is said. After a while GANDIL walks slowly over to CICOTTE at the pitcher's mound. Long pause)

GANDIL

Hit him right in the head.

CICOTTE

Think he's okay?

GANDIL

Sure. He's getting up now.

WEAVER

(Sarcastic)
Nice pitch. Great way to start the World Series.

JACKSON

Loosen up, Eddie!

WEAVER

All right, get this guy!

GANDIL
(To CICOTTE)
Take it easy.
(Goes back to first)

CICOTTE

Daubert has a good stick. Tough hitter. I better keep it away from him.

(CICOTTE winds up and throws. Pause)

WEAVER

Four straight balls. Great. First and second, nobody out.

(GANDIL walks to CICOTTE)

CICOTTE

How'm I doin'?

GANDIL

Don't make it too obvious. You can throw a strike
once in a while.

WILLIAMS
(TO MCMULLIN)
Cicotte's a jerk.

MCMULLIN

I think he has brain damage.

FELSCH

He keeps this up we're bound to get found out.

RISBERG

That's what I like to see. I hope they slaughter us.

(GANDIL goes back to first)

JACKSON

Concentrate, Eddie!

WEAVER

How 'bout it, Eddie?! Big strike out, kid!

WILLIAMS

Throw it in there, Eddie1 Go get him!

CICOTTE

First and second, nobody out. Groh's up. Big hitter
but I can strike him out. Maybe I better.

(Winds and throws. Pause)

WEAVER

Great. Hit him right in the back.

GANDIL
(Runs to mound)
Are you out of your fuckin' mind?

CICOTTE
It slipped out of my hand. I tried to strike him out.

GANDIL
Well start throwing some strikes. Don't be a moron.
Don't make it so obvious.

CICOTTE
I'm trying my best.

WEAVER
Get him out of there now. He's off.

WILLIAMS
(To MCMULLIN)
Come on, Eddie! Settle down!

JACKSON
This is garbage. To hell with them all, I'm playin' to
win.

(CICOTTE winds and throws. There is baseball banter all through the
next section. A hit to left that JACKSON throws to RISBERG, who
misses the tag. ALL PLAYERS react to the same action which is taking
place that the director will choreograph. Except GANDIL, who speaks
to the audience while the banter continues behind him)

GANDIL
Cicotte settled down after the first inning. We had
a one-one tie goin' into the fourth. I told Eddie we
had to fall behind so he just laid the ball in there for
them to hit. Cincinnati smacked the hell out of him
in the fourth inning. They scored five runs. Cicotte
got taken out of the game.

(CICOTTE walks to bench where HE is cajoled by WILLIAMS and MCMULLIN)

GANDIL (Continued)

Lefty didn't come on to pitch 'cause he was pitching tomorrow. Wilkinson pitched. Lucky for us he's not any good. We lost the game nine to one. Lefty pitched Game 2.

(WILLIAMS walks to mound and pitches)

GANDIL (Continued)

In the fourth inning he gave up three walks and Kopf hit a triple for three runs. We lost Game 2, four to two. Game 3 was a total disaster. We messed up bad. Dickie Kerr was pitching for us. It just didn't go our way. We won.

(ALL the PLAYERS are present the locker room. The World Series is in progress and this action is immediately following the third game. Chicago lost the first two ball games and have just won their first game in the Series. There is the feeling of false enthusiasm amongst the PLAYERS except for WEAVER, whose enthusiasm is genuine.)

WEAVER

That's one, fellas! Wow!

JACKSON

Good game.

FELSCH

We didn't deserve to win that game.

WEAVER

We did though!

GANDIL

Yes we did.

MCMULLIN

Only one error.

WILLIAMS

How many errors did we have?

MCMULL IN

Only one.

WILLIAMS

Seemed like a lot more.

MCMULLIN

There was.

CICOTTE

Dickie pitched a hell of a game.

GANDIL

Yes he did.

WEAVER

Kerr was outstanding!

FELSCH

We didn't deserve to win that game.

RISBERG

We shouldn't have won that game.

JACKSON

We did though.

WEAVER

Thanks to little Dickie Kerr. How many hits did he give up?

MCMULLIN

Three.

WILLIAMS

A three-hitter.

WEAVER

Outstanding!

CICOTTE

Outstanding.

GANDIL

Kerr did it all by himself.

JACKSON

We sure didn't help.

FELSCH

We got booed.

WEAVER

So what? We got booed before. We won, didn't we?

JACKSON

Fans are funny.

CICOTTE

They love you when you win and hate you when
you lose.

RISBERG

Shit on 'em.

WEAVER

What do you mean, shit on 'em? Fans are what
make this game.

JACKSON

They are.

RISBERG

We shouldn't have won that game.

WEAVER

But we did. Don't be so hard on yourself, Swede.

RISBERG

You asshole. I'm talking about . . .

WILLIAMS

Hey, we won a game we shouldn't have. It's no big deal. Sometimes the breaks go your way. The same could happen to Cincinnati tomorrow.

GANDIL

Yes it could.

CICOTTE

A three-hitter.

FELSCH

I don't like getting booed.

JACKSON

It's part of the game.

FELSCH

I guess so. But that guy didn't have to throw his peanuts at me.

MCMULLIN

You made an awful play.

WEAVER

You looked like a sandlotter.

GANDIL

He misjudged a fly ball. It's no big deal.

FELSCH

I should have caught it.

MCMULLIN
Dickie struck out the next two batters. Got us out of the inning.

CICOTTE
He was outstanding.

WILLIAMS
That was a nice throw from left field, Joe.

CICOTTE
Right on the money.

WEAVER
Swede should have had it.

JACKSON
It was a tough hop.

WEAVER
Yeah, waist high. Those are tough.

RISBERG
You got a problem, Weaver?

WEAVER
No, Swede, I don't. Nope. None at all.

FELSCH
Mr. Comiskey was pleased.

WEAVER
Yeah. He gave Dickie a big hug.

MCMULLIN
Kerr was all alone out there.

WEAVER
We'll get them again tomorrow.

FELSCH
(To WEAVER)
How's your new bat working out?

WEAVER
You tell me. Who got the first hit?

JACKSON
It was a good hit.

WEAVER
It was a great hit.

RISBERG
(To GANDIL)
We gonna be okay?

GANDIL
No problem. A lot of baseball is luck.

MCMULLIN
(In their conversation)
Sometimes there are powers beyond your control.

RISBERG
Go get hit by a train.

MCMULLIN
Temper, temper.

JACKSON
You're pitching tomorrow, right, Eddie?

CICOTTE
Yep.

WEAVER
How about a three-hitter.

CICOTTE

(Puzzled)
I'll do my best.

RISBERG

(To WEAVER)
Will you can it with all this rah-rah shit.

WEAVER

What are you talking about?

RISBERG

You know what I'm talking about.

WEAVER

I know what you're talking about?

RISBERG

You know what I'm talking about. Just can it.

WILLIAMS

Hey, Swede. Let's go get a drink.

RISBERG

Yeah. Let's get the hell out of here.

WILLIAMS

Where do you want to get a drink?

RISBERG

Anywhere.

WILLIAMS

Where do you want to go?

RISBERG

I don't know. Anyplace.

WILLIAMS

How about Stacey's?

RISBERG .

I hate that place.

WILLIAMS

Well, where do you want to go?

RISBERG

I don't know. Let's just get the hell out of here!

WILLIAMS

All right. Relax.

(WILLIAMS and RISBERG exit)

JACKSON
(To GANDIL)
You got something for me?

GANDIL

Not here. Not now.

JACKSON

Well, it's time.

GANDIL

I know. We'll make arrangements. You'll hear from me. Don't worry.

JACKSON

Well, make it soon.

GANDIL

It will be.

WEAVER

Swede's a strange guy. What's his problem?

CICOTTE

Bad childhood.

WEAVER

His adulthood's not so great either.

FELSCH

It's probably just the pressure of the World Series.
Some ballplayers just have a difficult time handling
the pressure. I think Swede's one of them.

WEAVER

He's played pretty lousy so far.

JACKSON

He'll come through.

CICOTTE

Joe, you want to go with me and Hap over to The
Palace Theater? Castle's got this redheaded dancer
who will knock your socks off.

JACKSON

No thanks, Eddie. I'm gonna head home, I'm
bushed.

CICOTTE

All right. We'll see you tomorrow then.

JACKSON

Right.

FELSCH

That guy threw peanuts at me.

CICOTTE

You'll get over it. I'll wait for you outside.

WEAVER

The way you looked on that play you're lucky he
didn't throw bricks at you.

FELSCH

Did it look that bad?

WEAVER

Awful, Hap. Just awful.

FELSCH

I'll have to work on it.

(FELSCH and CICOTTE exit. Pause)

WEAVER

We needed this win.

JACKSON

Yes we did.

WEAVER
(Sees MCMULLIN starting to leave)
Where you off to, Fred?

MCMULLIN

I don't know. Maybe I'll take a walk in the park.
It's a beautiful day.

WEAVER

Well , we'll see you tomorrow.

MCMULLIN

Yeah.

JACKSON

Hey, Mac. Nice double play today.

MCMULLIN

Thanks, Joe.
(MCMULLIN exits.

GANDIL, WEAVER and JACKSON are left alone on the stage now.
THEY slowly walk towards the audience and the next section is
done without being aware of each other. THEY speak directly to the
audience.)

JACKSON

Dickie Kerr pitched a hell of a game. We played
terrible today and still won. He was amazing.

GANDIL

I knew we should have gone after Kerr also. The
son of a bitch won the fuckin' game all by himself.
We were supposed to lose.

WEAVER

I'm gonna shorten up on my swing tomorrow. I'm
trying to crush the ball. I'll just try to meet it. I
lead the Series in batting. I have to brush up on my
fielding.

GANDIL

I have to talk to Lefty about Weaver. I don't think
he's earning his money. This rah-rah stuff is fine
but he has to produce more on the field. Yeah, he's
made some errors but I don't think they were very
important.

JACKSON

Speaking of producing. You better come up with
some cash real quick, Chick. Don't you try to pull
a fast one. I know you got Swede. But he's only
one guy. I admire Buck's attitude toward the whole
thing. Making out like everything is hunky-dory.
Putting on all these airs like everything is normal.
Maybe that's the best way.

WEAVER

If I have a good Series maybe I can get a bit more money next year. I have to show Comiskey I'm a valuable part of this team. (To OTHERS) I'm gonna hit the road. We'll get 'em tomorrow. Even this Series up. We're only down two games to one.

JACKSON

Right, Buck.

WEAVER

You coming, Joe?

JACKSON

Sure, I'll head down with you.

WEAVER

Great. Take it easy, Chick.

GANDIL

Yeah.

JACKSON
(As THEY're leaving)
I want to see some cash real quick, Chick.

GANDIL

You'll see it. You'll see it.

JACKSON

I better.

WEAVER
(As THEY're leaving)
What was that all about? Chick owe you some money or something?

JACKSON
(Laughing)
Nothing, Buck. Nothing.

(JACKSON and WEAVER exit. GANDIL is all alone now. HE picks up his bags. Talks to the audience again)

GANDIL

You know, it's all getting real interesting. I'll see what they want us to do tomorrow . . . if you have any extra cash . . . I'd put it on Cincinnati.

(GANDIL exits)

BLACKOUT

Scene 2

ALL are present once again in the locker room. It is after the last game of the Series. Chicago has lost. THEY are packing up for the off-season.

WEAVER

I don't understand.

JACKSON

Tough game.

WILLIAMS

We won the pennant. That ain't so bad.

WEAVER

We're better than those jerks.

MCMULLIN

We were big favorites.

WEAVER

That's 'cause we're better.

FELSCH

We'll get 'em next year.

WEAVER

We played like shit.

CICOTTE

Yes we did.

GANDIL

We did our best.

CICOTTE

We did, huh?

GANDIL

Yes we did.

WEAVER

If that was our best then we stink.

WILLIAMS

You can't win them all. We won the goddam
pennant, didn't we?

WEAVER

That's not enough.

CICOTTE

No it's not.

FELSCH

Comiskey was pissed.

CICOTTE

Wouldn't you be?

JACKSON

I didn't like the way he looked at me.

CICOTTE

How'd he look at you?

JACKSON

Like he knew something.

WEAVER

Yeah, he knew something. He knew we stunk.

GANDIL

Don't worry about it.

CICOTTE

We didn't play well.

WEAVER

That's brilliant, Eddie.

CICOTTE

I mean, we could have played a lot better.

JACKSON

Sure we could have.

FELSCH

We know that.

WEAVER

It's a little late now.

WILLIAMS

We won the pennant.

JACKSON

Good Series, Buck.

WEAVER

Don't matter. We didn't win.

JACKSON

Yeah, well, you know.

MCMULLIN

We were big favorites.

FELSCH

Comiskey knew that.

GANDIL

He's an owner. They all think you're big favorites.

CICOTTE

We let him down.

RISBERG

Bullshit. If he don't like the way I play, shit on 'em.

CICOTTE

He pays your salary.

RISBERG

I did my best.

GANDIL

We all did our best.

CICOTTE

Sometimes I think you believe that, Chick.

GANDIL

I do believe it. And you better believe it too.

WEAVER

We coulda done better.

CICOTTE

We shoulda done better.

JACKSON

Coulda, shoulda. We didn't, did we?

GANDIL

It's only a game.

CICOTTE

It's my job. I get paid for it.

GANDIL

And you got paid pretty well.

WILLIAMS

Forget about it. It's over. It's all water under the
bridge.

CICOTTE

It's not so easy to forget about it, Lefty.

GANDIL

Well, make it easy.

RISBERG

Yeah, make it easy.

WEAVER

Well, I know one ballplayer who's going to get
plowed tonight.

JACKSON

I could go for a few good belts myself.

WEAVER

I still don't understand. Cincinnati doesn't belong on
the same field as us.

FELSCH

Dickie played well.

JACKSON

Dickie's a ballplayer.

WILLIAMS

We all played well.

FELSCH

What are you going to do this winter, Joe?

JACKSON

Lots of hunting. It relaxes me.

FELSCH

That's great. Good Series, Joe. What did you end
up batting? .375?

JACKSON

Yeah. I got lucky.

GANDIL

Yeah. He got lucky.

FELSCH

What are you gonna be doing with yourself, Eddie?

CICOTTE

I got this new farm. I'll be doing a lot of work on it.

FELSCH

You got any horses?

CICOTTE

Not yet. Just some chickens and a few cows.

JACKSON

How do your kids like it?

CICOTTE

They love it. You should see them jump out of bed
in the morning to do their chores. They love to milk
the cows.

JACKSON

Kids love to milk cows.

WEAVER
I think I'll find me some cow to milk tonight.

WILLIAMS
What's the matter, Buck? You don't like pigs anymore? What's her name? Miriam?

WEAVER
She's a nice girl.

WILLIAMS
Sure, if you like fat.

WEAVER
She's not that big. She's just athletic.

WILLIAMS
What is she, a shot-putter?

WEAVER
No. She's a swimmer.

WILLIAMS
A swimmer, huh? Well, she better stay out of the ocean before someone harpoons her.

FELSCH
You played real good, Mac.

MCMULLIN
I tried.

FELSCH
It showed.

CICOTTE
(To JACKSON)
You really think Comiskey knew something?

JACKSON

I don't know. Maybe it's just my imagination. He looked at me awfully strange though.

CICOTTE

I hope it is just your imagination.

RISBERG

I'm gonna take my three grand and find me an all-night poker game and raise on every hand.

WEAVER

(TO JACKSON)

Joe, does Comiskey ever give bonuses before the season's over?

JACKSON

Never gave me one. Why, Buck?

WEAVER

Something strange I found this morning. Never mind, it's not important.

WILLIAMS

(To MCMULLIN , who s leaving)

Fred, wait up. Let's go get a drink.

MCMULLEN

All right. Have a good winter, guys? It wasn't meant to be this year.

FELSCH

Take care of yourself, Fred.

(OTHERS ad lib goodbyes)

WILLIAMS

Stay in shape this winter, girls.

(To GANDIL)

Piece of cake.

(THEY shake hands. OTHERS ad lib goodbyes. WILLIAMS and MCMULLEN exit)

                    WEAVER
I feel like shit.

                    CICOTTE
I feel awful too.

                    JACKSON
It'll pass.

                    WEAVER
I don't like to lose.

                    FELSCH
Everybody does some time, Buck.

                    RISBERG
        (TO GANDIL)
I'll see you soon, partner.
        (THEY shake)

                    RISBERG (Continued)
Enjoy your winnings.

                    GANDIL
Keep in touch.

                    RISBERG
You got it.

        (HE starts to leave)

                    FELSCH
Have a good winter, Swede.

RISBERG
(Without looking back)
Oh, I will.

(RISBERG exits)

CICOTTE
Risberg's a strange guy.

WEAVER
Calling Swede strange is a compliment.

CICOTTE
He don't seem to care.

WEAVER
He don't.

FELSCH
I'm gonna go, Eddie.

CICOTTE
I'm sorry, Hap.

FELSCH
Sorry for what?

CICOTTE
Sorry for everything. You know . . .

FELSCH
Don't worry about it.

CICOTTE
Will I see you this winter?

FELSCH
I don't know. I'm gonna be pretty busy. See you
next year, fellas.

JACKSON

So long, Hap.

(OTHERS ad lib goodbyes. FELSCH exits. As in the other scenes, the FOUR PLAYERS still Onstage talk to each other and also talk directly to the audience)

CICOTTE
(To audience)
I've been a nervous wreck. I should have never gotten involved. I'm not made up for this stuff. I don't know why I did. If Comiskey knows ...

GANDIL
(To audience)
It all went as smooth as silk. Everybody's happy. Everybody's paid. It was so easy it was disgusting. I'm surprised it hadn't been done long ago. Come to think of it maybe it has. Philadelphia got blown out a few years back. I wonder . .

CICOTTE
(To audience)
I don't know if I can hold out. I mean . . .

JACKSON
I didn't get all the money I was promised. Gandil assured me it's coming. It's over. We did it. That's it for me, though. I'm not very proud of myself . . .

WEAVER
Strange thing happened to me this morning. In my locker was a thousand dollars in a small envelope. I figured it came from Comiskey. You know, he gave me part of the winners' share even though we lost, for having a good Series. After the game I went over to him and said thanks. He said "What for?" I said "the money." He sort of looked at me pissed off-like and said "you earned it."

GANDIL

I think I'll get myself a racehorse. That's where the big money is. I think I might have found my calling. I have a knack for this.

CICOTTE

I wonder if these other guys feel like I do. How couldn't they? They're human, aren't they?

WEAVER

I don't want to tell the other guys about the money. You know, they might get mad at Comiskey for not giving them all some. They did their best. They were pretty lousy, though.

JACKSON

I just have this feeling in my gut that it's not over yet. I can't explain it. Maybe it was the way Comiskey looked at me. Like he knew something I didn't know . . .

GANDIL
    To OTHERS)
See you girls next year. Pleasure doing business with you.

CICOTTE

Guess you won't have trouble sleeping tonight, Gandil.

GANDIL

No I won't, Cicotte. I'm gonna sleep like a baby. Like a baby.

(GANDIL exits)

WEAVER

I'm gonna go get drunk.

JACKSON
Hang on, Buck. I'll go with you.

WEAVER
Sure, Joe .

JACKSON
(To CICOTTE)
You okay?

CICOTTE
I think so.

WEAVER
Don't take it so hard, Cicotte. We'll get 'em next year.

CICOTTE
Will we?

WEAVER
No doubt.

CICOTTE
If you say so.

WEAVER
Let's go, Joe.

JACKSON
Have a good winter, Eddie.

CICOTTE
You too, Joe. 'Bye, Buck.

(JACKSON and WEAVER exit.

CICOTTE is left all alone Onstage. HE grabs his stomach in pain. HE is obviously upset. HE addresses the audience)

CICOTTE (Continued)
It all happened so fast. I will never do this again.
That is a promise. I will never do this again . . .

BLACKOUT

Scene 3

As the scene opens we see GANDIL and RISBERG talking together in the locker room. WILLIAMS and MCMULLIN are also there. It is now one year later than the first six scenes. It is the fall of 1920.

RISBERG
This investigation shit has got me spooked.

GANDIL
Don't worry about it.

RISBERG
Comiskey's throwing a lot of dough into this thing.

GANDIL
I'm clean. How 'bout you? I didn't do anything.

RISBERG
I didn't do anything either.

WILLIAMS
I heard they're gonna talk to some guys from
Brooklyn and Philadelphia.

GANDIL
So some guys from Brooklyn get nabbed for
collecting a few bets. So what?

RISBERG
Well, it could get sticky, that's all.

GANDIL

Well, I didn't do anything. Did you, Lefty?

WILLIAMS

No, sir.

GANDIL

Did you, Swede?

RISBERG

No, I didn't do a thing.

GANDIL

How 'bout you, Fred? Did you do anything wrong?

MCMULLEN

With what?

GANDIL

Exactly my point. You guys get my meaning?

WILLIAMS

Right

RISBERG

Just keep our mouths shut.

GANDIL

That's right. We didn't do nothing. Comiskey's
just pissed off we lost last year's World Series. So
he's making all this noise in the papers that he's
conducting some in-house investigation into some
rumors about World Series fixing going on and that
he'll get to the bottom of it if it's the last thing he
does. It's all bullshit.

RISBERG

That's right.

GANDIL
He can't prove a goddam thing.

RISBERG
There's nothing to prove.

GANDIL
That's right.

WILLIAMS
It's been a long year.

MCMULLIN
I hear they're looking into a game with the Cubs and Philadelphia. They think it was fixed.

GANDIL
Probably was. It's happening all the time.

RISBERG
You think so?

GANDIL
I know so.

MCMULLIN
Well , there's talk that last year's World Series was brought up.

GANDIL
You guys are like little girls. We didn't do anything wrong. There's no crime.

WILLIAMS
If they want to get you on something they'll find something.

GANDIL

Why would they want to get us on something? Will
you guys use your heads. They're going to conduct
an investigation. That's proper. But they're not
going to find anything wrong. Then everybody will
be happy. The rumors will stop. Then we can get
on with baseball. They're not going to bite the hand
that feeds them. Comiskey's life is baseball. You
think he's going to dirty it?

WILLIAMS

You got a point.

GANDIL

Believe me. In a few weeks this whole thing will be
blown over. You won't hear another word about it.

RISBERG

You're right , Chick.

WILLIAMS

Let's just hope so.

(FELSCH enters)

MCMULLIN

How's it going, Hap?

FELSCH

I think we've got some problems.

MCMULLIN

What's wrong?

FELSCH

I just spoke with Joe. He says Eddie went to
Comiskey.

GANDIL

Yeah, so?

FELSCH

Well, Joe seems to think he told him all.

WILLIAMS

About what?

FELSCH

You know.

WILLIAMS

Shit.

GANDIL

Wait a second. What did Joe tell you?

FELSCH

Joe says that Eddie told him that he couldn't take
it anymore and that he went to Comiskey and
confessed.

RISBERG

I'll kill that little shit.

WILLIAMS

You're kidding?

MCMULLIN

I can't believe it.

GANDIL

Asshole. What exactly did he tell him?

FELSCH

I'm not sure. You'll have to ask him.

GANDIL

Oh, I'll ask him all right.

RISBERG

I swear I'm gonna rip his tongue out of his mouth.

WILLIAMS

Why would Cicotte do that?

FELSCH

He always had a hard time dealing with it.

WILLIAMS

But he's not alone in this thing. There are other people involved.

RISBERG

Little dandy shit. I'll fix it so he won't be doing much talking. I swear to God that I'm gonna rip his tongue out.

GANDIL

Calm down, Swede. We don't know what he said. We'll just wait till we get his side of the story.

FELSCH

Joe seemed pretty certain. Joe's a little scared.

MCMULLIN

What are we gonna do?

WILLIAMS

I can't believe it. Is he crazy?

MCMULLIN

What are we gonna do?

RISBERG

Yeah, Chick. What are we gonna do?

FELSCH

I don't think there's much we can do.

RISBERG

There's got to be something.

GANDIL

Everybody, relax. We don't know anything yet.

MCMULLIN

It's over, we're dead.

WILLIAMS

Unbelievable.

FELSCH

It was bound to happen.

GANDIL

Nothing's over. We didn't do nothing.

(JACKSON and CICOTTE enter)

RISBERG

Hey, Cicotte.

(Takes CICOTTE to front of locker as RISBERG and GANDIL look over him.)

RISBERG (Continued

Don't you have something to tell us?

CICOTTE

What do you mean?

RISBERG

You know what I mean. Heard you went to Comiskey.

WILLIAMS

It's not true, is it, Eddie?

GANDIL
What's the story, Cicotte?

CICOTTE
I did go to Comiskey.

RISBERG
What did you talk about?

CICOTTE
I told him.

GANDIL
How much?

CICOTTE
Everything.

GANDIL
Did you mention anybody else?

CICOTTE
Yes.

(RISBERG leaps at CICOTTE, grabs him and throws him up against the lockers. Bedlam follows as THEY ALL say the following during a massive fight)

CICOTTE (Continued)
Get your hands off me.

RISBERG
I'll kill you!

JACKSON
Swede! Swede!

GANDIL
Rip his tongue out, Swede! Rip it out!

RISBERG
You want some too, Jackson?

(RISBERG has lost it. HE is like a wild animal swinging at anything
that walks in his way. There is a lot of improvisation during the whole
fight. HE is on top of CICOTTE with his hand down his throat,
trying to grab his tongue)

FELSCH
He has a right to say what he wants.

(GANDIL joins in the mayhem. ALL THE PLAYERS are just reacting
to the fighting around them by fighting back themselves)

GANDIL
Shit on you, Felsch. It's my life he's fuckin' with!

(The fight turns out in essence to be GANDIL, RISBERG and
WILLIAMS against CICOTTE, JACKSON and FELSCH. MCMULLIN
is just trying to break things up. RISBERG cannot be stopped. HE is
jumping from ONE PLAYER to the NEXT trying to kill CICOTTE)

GANDIL (Continued)
Why didn't you just keep your mouth shut!

WILLIAMS
You asshole!

MCMULLIN
Hey! Hey! Hey!

(MCMULLIN is desperately trying to get EVERYONE'S attention.
HE is yelling louder and louder in the middle of the PACK OF BODIES
crawling around each other. The scene looks like a group of sixth grade
boys fighting after school. A lot of hugging and wrestling and missed
punches.

JACKSON has RISBERG from behind with his arm strangling his neck
telling him to calm down.

MCMULLIN is getting through as THEY are getting it all out of their system. The fight is beginning to settle down)

> MCMULLIN (Continued)
> EVERYBODY! Hey! Will you stop! Hey!
> You guys! Come on!

(MCMULLIN stands, frustrated, cups his hands around his mouth and yells as loud as HE can)
> COMISKEY'S COMING!!!!!

(For a second EVERYONE freezes. THEY slowly try to get to their feet and straighten themselves up. THEY look at MCMULLIN. THEY are ALL exhausted. There are still some exchanges but they are the exchanges of the end of a fight when all parties have had enough)

> MCMULLIN (Continued)
> He's not. But I had to get your attention.

> RISBERG
> (To CICOTTE, pointing)
> You're dead.

> CICOTTE
> Up yours, Risberg.

> JACKSON
> Enough, Swede.

> WILLIAMS
> Why did you squawk?

> FELSCH
> It doesn't matter.

> WILLIAMS
> Yes it does.

> RISBERG
> You've had it, you little piss hole!

JACKSON
I said that's enough.

GANDIL
So tell us, Cicotte. What did you tell him?

CICOTTE
I told him everything.

WILLIAMS
Did you tell him about us?

CICOTTE
I'm sorry, Lefty. I did.

RISBERG
You're sorry.

GANDIL
You just ruined it, Cicotte. It was perfect and you ruined it. Well, I'm not saying a goddam thing. I didn't do nothing. And if the rest of you are smart you'll keep your mouths shut too.

JACKSON
It's too late, Chick.

GANDIL
Not for me.

WILLIAMS
Why did you do it, Eddie?

FELSCH
It doesn't matter.

WILLIAMS
Yes it does.

FELSCH

What's the point? It doesn't matter.

RISBERG

I want to know too. Why the hell did you do it,
Cicotte?

JACKSON

What's the difference?

WILLIAMS

I'd like to know. It matters.

MCMULLIN

IT DOESN'T MATTER!

(THEY ALL look at him)

MCMULLIN (continued)

WE DID IT! GODDAM IT! WE DID IT!

(Pause)

CICOTTE

I couldn't live with myself, Lefty. I'm sorry if I got
you involved but I just couldn't go on anymore.
Maybe the rest of you can just act like nothing
happened but I couldn't sleep at night. What we did
was wrong, Lefty. Yeah, we got some money but we
broke the trust that lots of people had in us. It was
wrong. No matter what you say or how you act. It
was wrong. That's why I talked.

GANDIL

It was wrong? It was wrong, huh? Who made
you the almighty judge? Who said you make that
decision? Tell me something, Eddie. Did you ever
go into a grocer and get too much change and not
give it back?

CICOTTE

I don't think I know what you're . . .

GANDIL

Answer me! Did you ever get too much change?

CICOTTE

Yeah, of course I have.

GANDIL

Well, that's wrong, see. Did you ever go into a store
and have two pairs of pants in your bag and the guy
only charges you for one?

CICOTTE

I don't think I . . .

GANDIL

Answer the goddam question!!!!

CICOTTE

Yeah.

GANDIL

Well, that's wrong, see!!! Where do you draw the
line?! What is it, ten bucks? A hundred? Two
hundred? A thousand maybe?! Who the hell are
you to make that decision!!!!

CICOTTE

You're a tough guy, Gandil.

RISBERG

I don't need your guilt, Cicotte.

GANDIL

I'm not saying shit. As far as I know I never heard
of Eddie Cicotte.

FELSCH

It's okay, Eddie.

WILLIAMS

What are we gonna do?

GANDIL

You're on your own.

RISBERG

It's every man for himself.

GANDIL

Eddie just went and changed the rules. I can't help
you.

WILLIAMS

Well, we better think of something.

(WEAVER enters)

WEAVER

Hey, what the hell is going on? I just read in the
Tribune that Eddie's going before the Grand Jury
tomorrow.

BLACKOUT

Scene 4

This scene takes place during the Grand Jury investigation. As we view the scene we see CICOTTE, JACKSON and WEAVER in the Downstage area. GANDIL, RISBERG, WILLIAMS and MCMULLIN are in the Upstage locker room area. The PLAYERS in the Upstage area are not before the Grand Jury. The PLAYERS in the Downstage area are seated on chairs. When THEY speak it is straight ahead as if THEY were answering questions thrown at them from a prosecutor. The Upstage PLAYERS interact between themselves.

RISBERG

There's no crime.

WILLIAMS

They found something. I told you they would and they did.

MCMULLIN

What the hell is it again?

WILLIAMS

Conspiracy to commit an illegal act.

RISBERG

Where the hell did they find that one?

WILLIAMS

They found it.

RISBERG

Conspiracy, my ass. The whole goddam league is doing it. They're just using us.

MCMULLIN

Are we the only ones involved?

WILLIAMS

According to the bigwigs.

MCMULLIN

What can they do to us?

WILLIAMS

The maximum penalty is one to five years and a fine
of not more than ten thousand dollars.

MCMULLIN

Ten thousand dollars.

WILLIAMS

You got it.

RISBERG

I'm not saying nothin' to nobody.

WILLIAMS

It doesn't matter. If enough guys mention us it's the
same as if we took the stand.

MCMULLIN

What about the other investigations? Those guys
from Brooklyn and Philadelphia?

WILLIAMS

They found no wrongdoing.

RISBERG

Bullshit .

WILLIAMS

Maybe.

MCMULLIN

I wish I knew what those guys were saying.

PROSECUTOR'S VOICE

Mr. Cicotte. In your statement you name Jackson,
Gandil, Risberg, Felsch, Williams, Weaver and
McMullin as being involved in this deal. Is that
correct?

CICOTTE

Yes.

PROSECUTOR'S VOICE

But, Mr. Weaver, Mr. Cicotte names you specifically.

WEAVER

He's a liar. I don't know a thing about this. I
don't know what you're talking about. I didn't do
anything.

PROSECUTOR'S VOICE

You were never given any money in Cincinnati?

WEAVER

Uh . . . well . . . listen to me. All I want to do is
play baseball. I've got to play baseball. They're
all wrong. I don't know why they're saying this.
I didn't do nothing. For God's sake, believe me.
You've got to believe me.

PROSECUTOR'S VOICE

Mr. Jackson. Why would a man of your reputation
get involved in a scheme like this?

JACKSON

You ever make a bet on a baseball game?

PROSECUTOR'S VOICE

Well . . . uh . . . it's not an issue here whether I've
made a bet.

JACKSON

Just curious.

MCMULLIN

(Upstage)

You see they got this new Commissioner of
Baseball. Some judge. What's his name? Saw a
mountain or something.

WILLIAMS
Kennisaw Mountain Landis.

MCMULLIN
Right. Probably some hanging judge. He said that
even if we were found innocent he would kick us
out of baseball.

WILLIAMS
Not only kick us out but if anyone was ever caught
playing baseball with us anywhere they would
never play organized baseball again. He wants us
blackballed.

RISBERG
He can't kick us out. Who the hell is he?

MCMULLIN
Maybe those guys aren't saying anything. Maybe
they had a change of heart.

PROSECUTOR'S VOICE
Mr. Jackson also names you, Mr. Weaver.

WEAVER
Joe did? Why would he do that?

PROSECUTOR'S VOICE
That's what we're asking you.

WEAVER
Hey . . . uh . . . Don't I get a phone call or
something? I'd like to talk to my lawyer.

PROSECUTOR'S VOICE
That's not necessary, Mr. Weaver. This is just a
Grand Jury.

WEAVER

Well, you guys are pissin' me off.

PROSECUTOR'S VOICE

Mr. Cicotte. Mr. Gandil and Mr. Risberg call you a
liar.

CICOTTE

I'm not surprised.

PROSECUTOR'S VOICE

Then you swear to God that the statements you've
made are correct?

CICOTTE

Yes.

RISBERG

Where does Comiskey get off suspending us?

WILLIAMS .

Without pay.

MCMULLIN

It's just til after the investigation.

WILLIAMS

I think we're done, Fred.

RISBERG

Did you read his statement? "The integrity of
baseball is at stake." Bullshit. It's more than just us
eight. This thing is big. Real big.

WILLIAMS

They've called me before the Grand Jury. I don't
know what I'm gonna do.

RISBERG

Shit on 'em.

PROSECUTOR'S VOICE

Mr . Jackson, didn't you realize what you were doing was wrong?

JACKSON

(Low)

Yes.

PROSECUTOR'S VOICE

I'm sorry, could you speak up please.

JACKSON

I said yes.

PROSECUTOR'S VOICE

Then why did you get involved?

JACKSON

I didn't think it was *that* wrong.

PROSECUTOR'S VOICE

Mr. Weaver, this could take a long time if you keep insisting you know nothing about this.

WEAVER

I've got the time. I could use something to eat though. You got any food around here? You gonna keep us here all day, least you could do is feed us.

WILLIAMS

You think they'll be easy on those guys because they talked?

MCMULLIN

I heard they were granted immunity by the prosecutors for testifying.

WILLIAMS

Yeah?

RISBERG

The pansies.

MCMULLIN
(To WILLIAMS)
You gonna go tomorrow?

WILLIAMS

Maybe.

RISBERG

You're a sucker if you do.

WILLIAMS

I don't want to go to jail. If they give me immunity
. . .

RISBERG

Chick said "No one's going to jail."

PROSECUTOR'S VOICE

Mr. Jackson. Mr. Cicotte names George Weaver
as being involved. Could you substantiate that
statement?

JACKSON

No I couldn't.

PROSECUTOR'S VOICE

But in your statement you claim Mr. Cicotte speaks
the truth.

JACKSON

That's right.

PROSECUTOR'S VOICE

Then why can't you substantiate Mr. Cicotte's
statement?

JACKSON

I don't sub nothing. I just don't call Cicotte a liar.

PROSECUTOR'S VOICE

I don't understand.

JACKSON

Well, you figure it out.

PROSECUTOR'S VOICE

So the eight of you went willingly into this deal all together. Is that right, Mr. Cicotte?

CICOTTE

That's right.

RISBERG

They're not getting nothing out of me. Shit on 'em.

MCMULLIN

It's all over.

WILLIAMS

Maybe I'll go talk to them tomorrow. I don't know.

PROSECUTOR'S VOICE

That will be all, Mr. Jackson. Thank you.

JACKSON

(As HE rises)
What's gonna happen to us?

PROSECUTOR'S VOICE

That will be all, thank you.

JACKSON

Right. Thanks. Hey, you never answered my question.

PROSECUTOR'S VOICE
What question was that?

JACKSON
You ever place a bet?

PROSECUTOR'S VOICE
You can go now, Mr. Weaver.

WEAVER
Fantastic. I'm goddam starving. So everything's straight, right?

PROSECUTOR'S VOICE
You can go now.

WEAVER
Right. Yeah. Thanks a lot. I just want to play baseball, you know?

PROSECUTOR'S VOICE
I think we're finished, Mr. Cicotte.

CICOTTE
Right.
(Rises)

PROSECUTOR'S VOICE
I would like to thank you for being so straightforward. You've done baseball and the Chicago White Sox organization a great service.

CICOTTE
Yeah.
(Pause)
Could I say one thing to all of you?

PROSECUTOR'S VOICE
Certainly.

CICOTTE

Go to hell.

BLACKOUT

Scene 5

GANDIL and CICOTTE are alone in the locker room.

CICOTTE

Gandil . . .

GANDIL

Don't.

CICOTTE

I just wanted to say . . .

GANDIL

Don't say anything.

CICOTTE

I don't expect you to understand why I talked.

GANDIL

Oh. I understand what you did, Cicotte.

CICOTTE

Well, it's over. It just seems stupid. No hard feelings?

GANDIL

Are you fuckin' kiddin' me Cicotte? Listen. Don't say another word. For your own good. Don't say anything else.

CICOTTE

You don't understand.

GANDIL

No, you don't understand, Cicotte. You don't
understand. I'm gonna explain it to you, Eddie. I'm
gonna explain it and maybe, just maybe, it'll sink in
to that big thick skull of yours. You see, this here
was perfect. Goddammit. I'm gonna paint a picture
for you, Eddie. I'm gonna tell you something that
you'll never hear come out of my mouth again. You
were the best pitcher in baseball. You devoted your
life into taking this little ball and throwing it as
hard as you could. How many hours did you work
on it? You can't count them, can you? You worked
on it until your goddam hands bled. And you were
the best. And you know what I say? So what?
Do you know what Comiskey says, Cicotte? So
what?! Goddammit! I got to stand out there on the
field every day and look up in the stands and I see
Comiskey passing out cigars and shaking hands with
all these fat cats . . . and it makes me crazy! 'Cause
he needs me, see. Comiskey needs me. Comiskey
needs you. Without us he's nothing! And I've got
to get dirty looks from him if I happen to have a bad
game?! How many people in the world can do what
I do? Does he remember that?! Goddammit! You
were having trouble with your farm, huh, Eddie?
How come you didn't go to Comiskey? 'Cause you
knew he wouldn't give you a goddam dime! The
man's got more money than God and he made it off
us! But I've got to beg for another couple of dollars
on every contract I sign! I've got to be made to feel
like a piece of slime to even suggest such a thing!!
Goddam you!! Well, I beat it, Eddie. This was
perfect and I beat it. If they weren't going to give
me a piece then I was gonna walk right up under
his face and take it. And I did. And all you had to
do was one thing. Keep your mouth shut. And you
could have rode off into your fairy tale world of

GANDIL (Continued)

signing autographs and having little kids yell your
name and all that. And you could have made some
money too. But you couldn't do that, Cicotte. Yeah,
all these guys ignore you? What did you expect,
Mr. Apple Pie, that the city of Chicago was gonna
give you a goddam ticker tape parade? These guys
ignore you? Yeah. 'Cause this is the real world and
you ruined their goddam lives! I hope wherever you
go and whatever you do, people ignore you. I hope
it eats at you. I hope it makes you goddam sick.
'Cause I don't care about you. Comiskey doesn't
care about you. None of them care about you.
'Cause you're a goddam loser!!

CICOTTE

You never did. That's just it, Gandil! You never did.
You never cared about me. What is all this bullshit?
I don't fit in. I know that. I've always known that.
You don't think I don't sense the way you guys
treat me? I hear the jokes! You ask Risberg to
go to the club, you ask Williams to go for a drink.
Did anybody ever ask me? All I can do is throw
a baseball. And I do that damn good! When you
fellas asked me to go along with yas to throw the
World Series, that was the first time you ever asked
me to do anything. And you didn't ask me 'cause
you cared about me. You asked me because I could
throw a baseball. But something's wrong with me.
I'm messed up. 'Cause I was so thrilled to be a part
of you guys that I went along with it. Everybody
went along with it. Joe, Hap. Everybody. Goddamit,
I love baseball, Gandil! And you ain't never gonna
understand that! Comiskey pays me money to do
something I love. I'm a lucky fella. And when I
take his money what I do is I give him my word that
I will be my best. And when people pay money to
see us play they expect us to be our best! Don't talk
to me, Gandil, about Comiskey needing me! You
needed me. You needed Joe. You needed all of us. I

CICOTTE (Continued)

got no more pains in my gut, Gandil. I'm sleeping at
night. I saved my farm. I squared myself with you.
Now I squared myself with Comiskey. Don't you
ever call me a loser.

(Exits)

BLACKOUT

Scene 6

ALL THE PLAYERS assume various positions on the stage in the locker
room

RISBERG
(Comes forward)
Well, I never said nothing to nobody. Years from
now, when people remember this they'll say,
"Risberg's my kind of guy. He wasn't no squealer.
He never talked." Where I grew up if you were a
squealer it was the lowest thing you could be. I
wasn't no squealer. People will remember that.

WEAVER
(Comes forward)
They'll see their mistake. They'll see it. When
they do they'll welcome me back with open arms.
There'll be a big apology. I know it will happen.
It's got to happen. I didn't do anything. No matter
what they say I know I didn't do anything.

FELSCH

(Comes forward)

I don't feel so bad for myself as I do for some of the other guys. I'll get by. When you do something crooked you're bound to get nabbed sooner or later. I read somewhere that it's not the good things in life that you learn from but the bad things. Maybe. Baseball's a great game. It's good for America. It should be protected. I just hope people forget about this. Fast.

MCMULLIN

(Comes forward)

I guess I'm just stupid. I could kick myself in the head for getting involved. I had everything to lose and I lost it. I just hope people forget about me. I hope I'm the one who they say, "What was that last guy's name again?"

WILLIAMS

(Comes foward)

I still don't know why we can't play baseball anymore. They said we couldn't play baseball anywhere. Anywhere. It's the only thing I know how to do. I'll bet you anything they knew that. Sorry. I shouldn't be betting on anything anymore . . . I'll find something else to do. I don't know what but I'll find something.

CICOTTE

(Comes forward)

These guys are the best bunch of guys I've ever played ball with. I'm proud to have known each and every one of them. We had the best team in baseball. Hap says that if it wasn't me who came forward someone else would have. I hope so. It's hard for me to figure out guys like Gandil. I don't know what makes them the way they are. But you look at any group of guys on any street corner and there'll be a Chick Gandil among them. They just seem to be there.

GANDIL
(Comes forward)
I don't feel bad about what happened. We took a
little money. So what? I'm not a criminal. I didn't
kill anybody. We're men playing a boys' game.
They don't want to admit it but this is a business.
They can call it a sport, and an American game and
all that crap but it's a goddam business. They're
not gonna stop it. For as long as the game's played,
it'll go on. You see, people always want something
more. They're like mules. All you need is a stick, a
string and a big enough carrot and they'll reach for
it. They'll go for it. You can bet on it.

JACKSON
(Comes forward)
I was coming out of the courthouse the other day
and a group of kids were waiting by the steps. One
little guy, cute as a button, had tears in his eyes and
yelled to me, "Say it ain't so, Joe." Right then I had
realized what I'd done. I looked at the kid and said,
"I'm afraid it is, son." I'll always remember his
face.

LOUDSPEAKER
Charles A. Risberg
Claude Williams
Fred McMullin
George A. Weaver
Oscar Felsch
Edward V. Cicotte
Arnold Gandil
Joseph Jackson

Charge: Conspiracy to commit an illegal act.
Verdict: Not guilty.

(There is a pause as we look at an empty locker room. Then the lights)

FADE TO BLACK

ACKNOWLEDGMENTS

My sincere gratitude to the following people who had both a tangible involvement and an inspirational connection to the creation of *Out!* The individuals know which camp they fall into. Without them, this play would never have happened.

Beacon Lanes NYC, Gregory Brennan, Peter Brennan, Stephen Brennan, Jackson Bryer, Max Charruyer, Maureen Chepiga, Stephen Chepiga, Paul Christie, Michael Countryman, Dan D'Agrosa, Brian Dennehy, John Dexter, Stephen Dougherty, Mitch Douglas, Glenna Freedman, Peter Frisch, Sara Garonzik, Gregory Generet, Shirley Herz, Dawn Hewins-Kelly, Henry Holt & Company, Danny Kelly, Arnie Mazer, Bill Mazer, Nancy McCall, Pat McCorkle, Frank McCourt, Steve McGraw, Jack Pardee, Matthew Penn, Howard Platt, Valerie Sandberg, Ira Schlosser, Tamara Tunie, The New York Historical Society, The New York Public Library, The National Baseball Hall of Fame, The Order of the Royal Muddahs, Warner Wolf.

ABOUT THE AUTHOR

Lawrence Kelly has divided his time between the arts and education. He attended the American Academy of Dramatic Arts, SUNY at Oneonta, Dowling College, Teachers College/Columbia University and the Bank Street College of Education. He holds A.O.S, B.S., M.S. and M.Ed. degrees. He was the General Manager of Steve McGraw's Cabaret Theater in New York, responsible for such hits as *Forbidden Broadway*, *Forever Plaid* and *A Couple of Blaguards*. After many years as an English and Drama teacher, he currently is a High School Supervisor for the Alternate Learning Center, a program for at-risk students in New York City. He lives with his wife on the Upper West Side of Manhattan. He has two grown daughters. He spends his summer vacation in Rockport, Massachusetts.